"Will..."
He laughed, as breathless as Katie.

"You said that—"

With his arms still tight around her, he bent to kiss her again, then stopped abruptly. They both turned at the sound of someone quite near.

"Kathleen, is that you?" It was Justin.

Katie pulled away, but Will placed an arm around her waist. Rather than struggle, she remained still. "Justin, I'm surprised to see you—"

"I can see that."

"But this...it isn't what it seems," Katie said in dismay.

"Isn't it?" asked Will quietly. He tried to look into her eyes, but she twisted away. "Katie, don't do this, please. If ever in your life there was a time for honesty, this is it."

Dear Reader,

The book you are about to read is a special kind of romance written with you in mind. It combines the thrill of newfound romance and the inspiration of a shared faith. By combining the two, we offer you an alternative to promiscuity and superficial relationships. Now you can read a romantic novel—with the romance left intact.

Inspirational Romances from Thomas Nelson will introduce you to exciting places and to men and women very much involved in today's fast-paced world, yet searching for romance and love with commitment—for someone to cherish and be cherished by. You will enjoy sharing their experiences. Most of all you will be uplifted by a romance that involves much more than physical attraction.

Welcome to a special kind of book with a special kind of love.

Etta Wilson
Etta Wilson, Editor

Lessons in Love

Patricia Dunaway

Thomas Nelson Publishers • Nashville • Camden • New York

For my daughter, Jeannie,
who loves her kids,
especially our sweet Sara

Copyright © 1984 by Patti Dunaway

All rights reserved. Written permission must be secured from the publisher to use or reproduce any part of this book, except for brief quotations in critical reviews or articles.

Published in Nashville, Tennessee, by Thomas Nelson, Inc. and distributed in Canada by Lawson Falle, Ltd., Cambridge, Ontario.

Printed in the United States of America.

Scripture quotations are from the New American Standard Bible, © The Lockman Foundation 1960, 1962, 1963, 1968, 1971, 1972, 1973, 1975, and are used by permission.

All of the characters and events in this book are fictitious. Any resemblance to actual persons, living or dead, or to actual events is purely coincidental.

ISBN 0-8407-7357-9

Chapter One

Spring seemed to be taking its time this year. It was raining again. Katie Holland watched from the shelter of the doorway, postponing the moment when she must step out into the gentle, insistent drizzle. Her reluctance was plain on her face—an interesting face but a bit too long to be actually beautiful. Nonetheless there was something in her wide greenish eyes and the curve of her mouth that was very fresh and appealing—honesty, or vulnerability, or maybe just a natural sweetness.

Katie sighed as she ran her fingers through her long, light brown hair and the honest, vulnerable sweetness was replaced by honest aggravation. *Not much curl left*. Cinching the belt of her khaki raincoat tighter, she was glad she'd at least remembered to bring her umbrella. She stepped outside the student union building, fighting the stubborn thing as always. Pretty and yellow and sunshine bright as it was, she had the suspicion that if umbrellas could think, this particular one would prefer not to open, ever, for her.

"I win this time!" she said breathlessly when it popped open above her shoulder.

"Hey, look out!" It was a man's voice, deep and very close.

Katie whirled and he ducked as the umbrella whizzed by. "Oh, I'm so sorry. Did I hit you?"

"You missed both eyes both times, but my nose may never be the same. Do you have a license to carry that weapon?"

He was so tall she had to look up into his eyes, which were blue and slightly wary at the moment. This was something new for Katie—not blue eyes, but someone tall enough to look up to. Katie looked a lot of people in the eye, young men included. And this man was not at all like most of her classmates. He was wearing jeans, as almost everyone else on the small informal campus did. But where most of the students just managed to look scruffy, his neat jeans were paired with a cream turtleneck and a buff corduroy jacket, for an attractive casual look. It wasn't just the fact that he was obviously older, either. No, there was something else that wasn't so easy to define, but it stirred her somewhere at the level beyond immediate analysis.

"I didn't really hit your nose, did I?" she asked faintly, hopefully.

He shook his head. "But it was close enough that I think you owe me shelter under that menace, if you're going the same direction, anyway." His grin was a quick, mischievous flash. "Maybe even if you're not."

"Well, I..."

"My name is Will Adams. I'm a teacher, and I'm usually pretty trustworthy, in case you're wondering."

His eyes were not only blue, they reminded Katie of the ocean, her beloved ocean. They were a little green, just a hint, but mostly blue. Determined not to show that she *had* been wondering, and more to the point, how flustered she suddenly felt, she tried to concentrate on something besides his eyes.

"I'm Katie Holland, and I'm going back to the gym. I hope you are too, because registration's almost over and I'm late already." She surrendered the umbrella to him as they moved down the steps. As he took the contrary yellow umbrella his hand brushed hers slightly. It was warm, as warm as hers was cold.

"Messed up your schedule, I take it."

"That's an understatement. Can you believe I signed up for Basic Meteorology 390?"

His face, sun browned and lean, had a knowing, amused look on it. "Thinking it was—"

"Art in the Elementary School 390. I'm not so anxious to take it, but I need the credits. Sometimes I think I'll never get through school, and even if by some miracle I do, things won't be that much better." At twenty-four Katie herself was older than many of the girls in her classes, having taken a round-about route to college. Irrelevantly she thought how nice it was to walk with someone who had longer legs than hers. She always had to adjust and take mincing steps when she walked with most people, especially her roommate Sharon. But not with this Will Adams, whose stride seemed to match hers quite well, and quite naturally.

During their brief, pleasant walk Katie viewed the familiar campus with fond eyes. The stately brick buildings and carefully tended grounds were especially beautiful to her because she loved old buildings and houses with stories and histories, and this campus had plenty of both. Parts of the school were over a hundred years old, built when it had been Oregon Normal School instead of a state college as it was now. She glanced at the man walking quietly beside her, wondering again about him.

A teacher, he'd said. Did that mean he was a professor, or a teacher here for more training, or what? Somehow he just didn't fit her idea of a teacher. He looked more like a cowboy minus his Stetson, or a captain without his ship, or...Katie scotched her fantasies firmly.

As he followed her up the stairs of the old gym he asked, "Why do you say things won't be much better? I take it you're studying to be a teacher." His hands, as brown as his face, had long, slender fingers with clean nails, and he managed to close the umbrella so easily it piqued Katie a little. The thing never behaved so well for her.

When she reached for the door handle he beat her to it, which was a pleasant surprise. Most of the young men she knew had stopped bothering with such niceties, although she had to admit Justin never forgot.

"Thank you," she said, glancing up at him, trying surreptitiously to see if perhaps she had, in fact, hit his nose. If she had, it wasn't damaged. It was a very nice nose, straight and well shaped, not too long. She also noticed that his dark hair curled slightly from the dampness, instead of straightening as hers did.

It was becoming ridiculously difficult to take her eyes from him, but she smiled and turned away as she said, "Yes, I am studying to be a teacher, but I'll probably be terrible at it. Last year in Contemporary Ed 111—you know, the one where you're actually in a classroom as a helper—well, I could have used the National Guard a couple of times."

"Discipline problems?"

"Right. I just don't know if I'm cut out to be a teacher." She slipped out of her raincoat and was glad she'd worn her new pink sweater, knowing it gave her face, normally a bit pale, a nice glow.

He looked directly at her with disconcerting intensity and his deep voice carried even over the noise in the large, crowded room as he said, "There are certainly enough poor teachers in the world. Why keep at it if you don't think you're suited for it?"

"Because..." Katie bit her lip, knowing the glow on her face now was from embarrassment, not the pink sweater. She could probably explain her mother's firm resolve that her only child get through college, but what about Justin? That was another matter altogether. Of course, Justin never came right out with it the way her mother did, but the meaning in his quiet, persistent encouragement to finish college was very plain. And there was another reason, which was even more private.

How could she tell this man with his disquieting intensity that somehow, even with all her doubts about her career, her dismal failures as a student, she felt God wanted her right where she was? No, she couldn't say those things to a stranger, especially one who seemed to grow more disapproving of her by the minute.

Instead she said, "If I don't see Dr. Johnson soon things are going to go from bad to worse. I...I'm glad to have met you." She glanced up at him, summoning a polite smile from somewhere.

His expression was thoughtful and he didn't reply—just nodded his head. She hurried away, a frown making a dent between her eyes. It wasn't as though she hadn't already thought about what he'd said. Maybe he was right—maybe she should reconsider and try something besides teaching. But she was almost half through the Elementary Ed program, and changing her major now was more than she could face.

Dr. Johnson, her faculty advisor, looked up from the pile of papers he was shuffling on the desk before him as she strode breathlessly up. "Katie! It's good to see you. Have you finalized your schedule yet?"

"Oh, Dr. Johnson, no. There was a mix-up, my mistake, as usual. I need to find something that will give me three credit hours. What do you suggest?"

He was a small, round man, and usually smiling. But now his face grew serious and he shook his head. "It's so late, but sit down, sit down. We'll go through and see what else is left."

She sank gratefully into the chair beside him, wishing this year could have been different. Every term she managed to make some colossal error, snarling her schedule beyond belief. Katie tried to relax as Dr. Johnson leafed through the papers on his desk, but when he gave a low exclamation she leaned toward him expectantly. "Did you find something?"

He was smiling again. "Yes, I believe I have. They badly need someone in the preschool."

"Preschool?" she asked doubtfully. "I've never thought about that. I'm not sure I could manage little ones." Growing up as an only child had its disadvantages. She had never been around babies or young children much.

"I really think you should consider it. The instructor is very good, I hear. New on staff this year, but as I say, he has excellent references. He comes from New Mexico, if I'm not mistaken. It could be a good experience for you, Katie, and besides, I'm afraid all the other field study classes are filled."

Katie hesitated, but realized there was not much else she could do. She couldn't afford not to have a full schedule. "All right, Dr. Johnson, sign me up."

"I should tell you that it's not the usual—" He broke off then, his hand raised in greeting.

Katie's face registered her dismay when she saw who Dr. Johnson was enthusiastically waving over—Will Adams. Though she quickly rearranged her expression, she knew he'd seen it.

"Mr. Adams! Come here, I want you to meet someone." Dr. Johnson beamed up at Will Adams, whose gaze shifted from the advisor to Katie. "This is Katie Holland, Will, and I was just telling her about you and your class, and that she's going to benefit enormously from it."

Katie felt her stomach sink, but she tried to smile as she said weakly, "You're the new teaching instructor at the preschool."

"Uh huh," he said, his eyes gazing directly into her own. "And do I understand you've signed up to assist me?" She nodded, and he went on, "That's interesting. May I ask why?"

Her face felt warm; she'd always blushed easily. But she lifted her chin and answered him firmly as possible, knowing from experience that telling the truth was easier than trying to think of a plausible fib. "Because Dr. Johnson persuaded me. I'd appreciate the opportunity, if it's all right with you."

"And you need the credits," he murmured. Dr. Johnson leaned forward to catch the soft words Will Adams added, "No doubt Miss Holland will find our situation...ah, challenging."

Dr. Johnson smiled benevolently at them both. "Excellent, excellent. I'm sure she'll be an asset to your classroom."

Will Adams only nodded, his shrewd glance resting briefly on Katie before he said a courteous good-bye to Dr. Johnson, then sauntered away. Katie sighed; it was going to be another long term.

At least the rain stopped and I don't have to fight this silly umbrella, she thought as she was walking home. The apartment Katie and Sharon Wilson, her roommate, had been lucky enough to find was on the third floor of what had once been a fine mansion, built many years ago by one of the area's founding fathers. When she turned the corner and caught sight of it, she smiled.

In her mind the wonderfully intricate gingerbread trim, the encircling spacious porches on the first floor, the graceful bay and round turret that held her bedroom on the third floor had all been lovingly planned for a beautiful young bride. She had imagined several fanciful, dreamy versions of the proud husband bringing his new wife to see it. The reality she'd unearthed in one of the county library's history books revealed a less romantic story. The wife had been a rich, grizzled old settler's third spouse; the house part of an agreement drawn up by the way-past-her-prime bride's father. Strictly business.

That's the attitude she was going to have to remember, to be very businesslike and serious, or Mr. Adams could make the term pretty miserable for her. He certainly hadn't seemed pleased to learn that she would be in his classroom this term. She sighed. Every term had its pitfalls, and each seemed to get harder. Katie had the feeling that Will Adams and his preschool might be the end of her. And if she didn't graduate, what was left? She'd endured secretarial school, only to discover too late that office work, day in and day out, was more than she could face—or even handle. Her first boss had discreetly allowed her to quit. Her second just told her that while she was a joy to have around, she was a luxury he couldn't afford. Becoming a teacher was her mother's idea, and it had seemed a good one at the beginning of last year.

Feeling depressed, she trudged slowly up the stairs. The hall was dim and she could smell someone's dinner cooking—probably the Maxwells', who lived on the whole second floor. At least Justin was taking her out to eat this evening. Katie liked to cook but she was tired, and Sharon considered herself a gourmet cook when she added a can of mushrooms to the ground beef. But she was a good roommate, except for the music. Katie could hear it now, even before she opened the door.

Sharon was in the window seat as usual, a book on her drawn-up knees, papers all around, and the tape deck beside her screeching three decibels over Katie's limit. From experience Katie knew better than to say anything; she just walked over and turned it down to a bearable level. The two had fought their way to a basic understanding about several things, the difference in their taste in music only one of them. Sharon's ran to Christian rock, which Katie declared was a contradiction, believing that Christian lyrics and a rock beat just didn't go together.

Aside from the *Nutcracker Suite*, which her mother liked and played every Christmas, Katie didn't have much musical background, but she had decided classical music was the only kind she could listen to over and over without tiring of it. She was now working her way through the romantic composers, and on a Chopin binge that drove Sharon up the wall—or sometimes out of the apartment. Katie's mother had promised to buy her earphones next Christmas.

"Hi, roomie," said Sharon, grinning. "You look beat. Is Justin, King of the Computers, coming tonight?"

Katie nodded, amazed as always at the vitality of the tiny young woman who was not only her roommate, but her friend as well. Even Justin, whose taste didn't run to haphazard girls like Sharon, admitted she had something. Though she was barely five feet tall, she managed to make the most of the only two physical assets she possessed—a pair of huge, melting gray eyes and a tiny, neat waist.

Despite the fact that her narrow body was flat as a boy's and the space between her front teeth was an orthodontist's nightmare and her hair looked as though it had been cut with pinking shears—which it had one night when Sharon wondered what it would look like—young men were always flocking about her. She kept them all at arm's length, though. She was firmly convinced that God had special men in mind for both of them. Sharon knew she hadn't found hers yet, and she wasn't at all sure Katie had.

Katie smiled. "Yes, Justin's coming tonight. He's taking me to dinner at Le Bistro in Salem."

"Mmmmm. Heavy artillery. Do you think he's going to propose?"

Katie sank into the chair she'd managed to persuade her mother she couldn't live without. It was a dark brown leather wingback that had been part of a very expensive set. She dodged Sharon's question. "He'll be here at six."

"Hey, it's after five now. You'd better get a move on. Are you going to wear that new, old-rose dress? Well, you know what I mean, your new dress that's such a pretty old-rose color." Katie nodded, head back, eyes closed.

"You don't seem too excited," said Sharon.

Katie put a hand over her eyes, not wanting to work up enthusiasm she didn't feel. "Oh, Sharon, sometimes I'm just not sure about things."

"By 'things,' you mean whether or not you should say yes when Computer Man pops the question."

"Don't call him that," Katie said, frowning. "One of these days you're going to forget and say it to his face."

Sharon gave her a wicked grin that said plainly, *you think I haven't already?*

"But Sharon, he's steady; he's a college graduate and has a marvelous job; he's good looking—"

"I'll grant you that," interrupted Sharon, "if you like the men's hairspray commercial type. *Per*-fect."

Katie decided to ignore that comment, mostly because it was uncomfortably accurate. "And he puts up with me."

Suddenly serious, Sharon swung her legs down; her feet barely touched the floor. "That's what bothers me about your relationship with Justin, Katie. The attitude that he's somehow better and finer than you are. It's just not true." She came to stand beside Katie's chair and placed her small hand with its bitten nails on her friend's shoulder.

"But Sharon, I'm never quite altogether. I'm too tall, my slip shows or I forget to wear one, or my hem comes out. My grades are average, maybe, if I work really hard. I'm clumsy. Did I ever tell you how Mom arranged for me to take gymnastics so I would be more graceful and I fell off the beam and broke my wrist? It was the low beam, too." She gave a heart-felt sigh. "I don't even have the coordination to play the piano or type. Forty words a minute with an error a line—that's tops for me even after a year and a half in business school. I just wish I was good at one thing."

"Sounds like you're feeling sorry for yourself to me, sweetie," said Sharon mildly.

Stung, Katie couldn't deny it. "Justin's even a Christian. He's everything I ought to want—"

"But where is it written that you *have* to get married, even if you are getting rather old?"

"Sharon!"

She smirked. "Girls used to think they were old maids at seventeen, and you're seven years beyond that, Katie." Her face grew serious again as she added, "I just think that if it comes to a choice between the wrong man and no man, a woman is better off with none, roomie. And can you say absolutely that Justin is God's choice for you?"

"Oh, I—" There was a knock at the door then, and even though she knew it was Justin and she knew she was going to be late, again, Katie was glad not to have to answer that question. She flew to her room, making signs to Sharon to answer the door and keep him entertained while she dressed.

Le Bistro was a new restaurant, very elegant and quiet. Katie looked around and decided the room definitely had a French Provincial atmosphere, with old lace at the windows, carefully tended pots of deep pink geraniums on black iron racks, and mellow red brick walls. There were fresh-cut flowers at the linen-covered table, and the silver and crystal were just that, real silver and crystal. Justin liked nice things and had said more than once, with meaning heavy in his voice, that his home would be furnished with nothing but the best.

Knowing Justin liked to choose for both of them, she asked him to order dinner. They had *medallions de boeuf* and *champignons sauvage*—translated, steak with wild mushrooms, fresh asparagus, and a salad of endive so artfully arranged Katie hated to eat it. Dessert was a simple flan, but garnished with fresh strawberries, peaches, and pale green Kiwi fruit and lightly glazed with something that tasted sinfully good. Sharon would definitely say he was bringing out the heavy artillery if Katie found the nerve to tell her what they'd eaten.

As they finished the meal Katie sighed inwardly, recalling how she and her mother had saved to get her through that first year of college. There certainly hadn't been any extra money for restaurants like this one.

"Mom would like it here," she said, because she realized Justin had been watching her closely and was probably wondering why she'd been so quiet all through dinner.

"We'll have to bring her with us next time."

"Oh, Justin, it's too expensive."

He shook his head. "You keep forgetting, I like to spoil my women."

She couldn't resist teasing him. "You sound as though you have a harem."

"You know better than that. There's no one but you, Kathleen," he said seriously. In the flickering candlelight she could read something in his gray eyes that made her restless. She swallowed uneasily, and tried to think of a safer topic of conversation.

"That was a lovely dinner, Justin," she said with complete honesty and smiled at him across the table. The dark, well-tailored, three-piece suit he wore perfectly complemented his immaculate good looks. He had thick, light hair, styled and blow-dried expertly, and his fond gaze was warm.

"I'm glad you enjoyed it. Thought you might need something special after registration. By the way, how did it go?" With an almost imperceptible wave of his hand he signaled the waiter, who hurried over to their table. Waiters always came immediately when Justin signaled. He asked for the check, then continued as though she had told him about the whole wretched mix-up, which was probably just as well. "I can remember how it was, making sure you have all the right classes and the right profs—now that's important. How did you do there?"

"Fairly well, I think. There's a new one, a Will Adams."

"I don't recognize the name."

"Oh, you wouldn't. He's in the preschool."

"Preschool?" He frowned. "I didn't know you were interested in that age."

Katie decided to brazen it out. "It just seemed like a good idea to get the experience, and my advisor says Adams is marvelous with the children." She would have preferred telling Justin what had really happened, being able to laugh and feel better about it instead of pretending the whole thing wasn't an accident. But she knew Justin wouldn't think it was funny, so with an acute sense of her hypocrisy, she just said, "I'm looking forward to working with him."

"You've met him, then?"

"Yes, this afternoon." She certainly wasn't going to mention the fact that she'd met him at the point of her umbrella. Another lecture, even a loving one, on carelessness would make a terrible end to a hard day. "I suppose he will have a lot to teach me."

"No doubt. I just wish you'd consider changing schools. It would be so much nicer if we were closer."

"Now Justin, we've been all through that. Besides, it's only twenty miles to Salem, and I like it where I am. Sharon and I have the apartment fixed the way we want it, and after almost two years I feel I've invested a lot in my friends and in the school in general. I like it," she repeated a little stubbornly.

"I know, I know," he soothed. "But a degree from the university would be so much more desirable."

"And impressive?" There was a quiet warning in her voice.

He obviously received her full message because he reached for her hand across the table. "I'm sorry. It's just that I want the best for you, Kathleen, I really do. I care about you, and want to—"

She cut in, something she didn't do often. "Justin,

could we go now? I'm really tired. Classes start tomorrow, and it's going to be another full day."

"Of course." He rose to pull out Katie's chair. His hands lingered on her shoulders as he carefully arranged the soft angora sweater that had been his birthday gift last year. "It's been a nice evening, Kathleen. There's no one I like being with more than you..."

He trailed off and though Katie knew he wanted her to say the same, or more, somehow she couldn't. But she could smile, and she made it as warm as possible when she stood and turned toward him. She saw with dismay that from the look on Justin Moore's face he read a great deal more into her smile than she intended.

Later as they stood close at the door to her apartment she was sure her intuition had been right. Justin was saying, "You're so sweet." His hand moved gently on the back of her neck to bring her even closer. He was only an inch or so taller than Katie, but he was well proportioned. His shoulders were broad, but not too broad—a very well put-together man indeed.

She swayed toward him, eyes closed, aware of the warm strength of his body, the touch of his lips on her own, the smell of light, expensive aftershave. It was a very nice place to be. But when he held her even tighter, and his kiss grew deeper, she felt a small, inexplicable panic and pulled away.

"I...I'd better go in. It was a wonderful evening, Justin." She couldn't quite interpret the look in his eyes as he released her, but the note of regret in his voice was plain.

"Kathleen, I don't mean to rush you, but surely you know how I feel."

Katie stared for a long moment into his eyes, which were dark now with emotion. He was so fine, so quiet and good. She put her hand on his smooth-shaven cheek. He turned his head slowly and the kiss on her palm was whisper light, but a small shiver went through her body.

"Oh, Justin, I—" Whatever the right words were, they stuck somewhere in her throat.

His voice was very low and a little rough as he said, "It's all right. I'm a patient man." One last brush of his lips on her forehead, and he was gone.

She stood leaning against the door frame for a long time, not at all sure of the thoughts and feelings in her tired mind and heart. Then she slipped quietly inside and went directly to her own room, past the questioning look on Sharon's face. She just wanted to be alone, to try and sort out the day's events.

Chapter Two

Katie stood outside the door of the teaching resource room that had taken her ten extra minutes to find, and drew a deep breath. Even if she hadn't been late, the thought of facing Will Adams and a roomful of kids after last year's fiascos in the grade school classroom was enough to make her turn and run. But she resolutely pushed open the door and slipped in.

She was astonished to see a jumble of bright toys and unfamiliar equipment, tiny cribs built double-decker against the wall—and children. They ranged from only a few months in age to one little boy who might be as old as six, and most of them were far different than she'd expected. She had never been very good at hiding her feelings, but she tried hard to smooth out the shock she knew was plain on her face.

A dark-haired young woman sitting cross-legged on the floor rose gracefully and approached Katie. "Hi, I'm Ellen. I come in several times a week as a volunteer. This your first time?"

Katie nodded slowly. "My name is Katie Holland, and I—I didn't realize the children were..."

A quick look of sympathy flashed in Ellen's eyes. "You mean nobody explained about our kids?" She glanced to where Will Adams sat very close in front of a child who looked to be no more than a year old. Katie murmured something about signing up late yesterday afternoon and Ellen said anxiously, "That's too bad, someone should have told you. Does it...well, do you think it will bother you? It does some people, I guess. Not me, I just love 'em all to pieces."

"You mean that most of them are—" Katie stopped again; no appropriate word or phrase came to mind.

Ellen patted her arm. "The term we use is developmentally disabled. It's a catchall for conditions the kids have that range from Down's syndrome and cerebral palsy to things that nobody, not even the experts, can put a name to."

"Oh, I see," said Katie, not at all sure she did. Just then she felt someone patting her leg, much as Ellen had patted her arm. She looked down to see a wisp of a boy with a cleft palate marring his tea-colored face.

Ellen laughed. "Robby, you rascal, don't you ever get enough?" To Katie she said, "Go ahead, pick him up and ask him what he wants."

Katie knelt and took him into her arms. His fragile body reminded her of a baby bird she had once rescued from her dog. As she smiled into his enormous, solemn black eyes she said slowly, "What do you want, Robby?"

Ellen repeated the question, reinforcing it with sign language this time. After gauging Ellen's expression, Robby appeared to decide that if she wouldn't give in, he had to. The bunched fingers of both tiny hands came up to his face and made a little sweeping motion outward from his mouth three times.

"Cat?" said Ellen. He nodded, a delighted grin on his mouth. The cleft palate that prevented speech certainly didn't keep him from smiling. "You want to see Garbage Cat again?" She took Katie's arm and led her to the window where, just outside, a sleek black and white cat lay sunning himself on the rack built for garbage cans. The cat obligingly stretched, as though he knew he had an appreciative audience and began his morning grooming session. Ellen shook her head and smiled. "When Robby goes in for surgery he's really going to miss old Garbage Cat."

"Can they fix it?" Katie asked softly.

"Sure. They do wonders with cleft palates these days, and much earlier than they used to. He's only two, and they say he'll be talking a blue streak before we know it. I only wish all their problems were as easy to solve." She nodded toward the other children.

"Some of them seem, well, so normal," murmured Katie.

"Yes, they seem normal, and some of them do function pretty well. But they have problems communicating, or just learning, like Eddie." She inclined her head toward a chubby little boy who was laughing uproariously as one of the other volunteers read to him. "Come on, you need to see Will in action with Mark. He's terrific with all the kids." Katie followed her, still holding Robby in her arms.

Will glanced up only briefly. He gave a quick nod of recognition, then turned his attention back to the baby, who had a bad head cold. He laid his head to one side, pudgy fingers spread on the tray of the specially built chair in which he sat, his blue eyes looking tired.

"No, no, Mark, you aren't finished yet," said Will, his voice low and firm. "Pick up the blocks. Pick them up," he said, more slowly this time. Mark gave Will a tiny smile, but his hands were still and he made no move to pick up the blocks on the tray before him. "Now come on, you can do it. One more time..." Will took two green blocks away and replaced them with two red ones. Slowly Mark lifted his head and grasped the blocks, one in each hand, as Will brought up a plastic bowl. "In here, Mark, drop them in here." When he did, Will put the bowl down and placed his hands on the baby's round little ears. "That's good, Mark, *good!*"

Katie heard the reproach in her voice but couldn't mask it as she said, "It doesn't seem right to make him work when he has a cold and doesn't feel well. How old is he, anyway?"

Will looked up at her, frowning slightly. "He's eleven months old, Miss Holland, and we have a lot of ground to cover. Sure, it's hard for him, but we believe the younger we begin with children like Mark the better chance they have to learn. As you can see, we have to teach them things a normal child would do naturally, and much sooner." He turned back and unstrapped Mark, picked him up and held him close. "And we have to work whether we feel like it or not, don't we, sweetpea?" Mark nestled his head into Will's shoulder.

Katie was touched in spite of herself at the sight of the tall, slim man cuddling the baby and the smile that came to her lips was genuine and warm. "You forgot to tell me that your classroom and kids were...so special."

He shrugged. "I guess I did, I'm sorry. But you've got the right idea. My kids are special, every one of them in their own way. Isn't that right, Robby?" He tickled the little boy in Katie's arms, and the child wriggled with giggles and pleasure.

Just then Katie felt a warm, wet spot on her arm and looked down in dismay. "Uh, oh, I think he's..."

Ellen joined Robby's giggling. "I think you've just been initiated! Come on, let's get you both cleaned up. I should have taken him sooner."

Telling herself to be a good sport, Katie glanced back at Will, but his attention was on Mark again, fully and completely. The man had a one-track mind. During the next hour Katie read to the delightful, brown-eyed, dimpled Eddie, who made the best audience of one she had ever had; kept an angry, thin-faced little girl named Julie from biting a chunk out of Mark's leg; and grew pleasantly deaf from the din of fifteen children in the relatively small room.

When Will Adams approached after a learning session with the dry-again Robby, she smiled gamely up at him. She was sitting in a rocking chair, Mark in her arms, still comforting him after Julie's unprovoked attack. With both hands stuck in the pockets of his jeans he asked, "Well, what do you think of things so far?"

"I'll be honest with you, Mr. Adams. It's different from anything I've ever experienced before..." She hesitated, then decided she might as well be honest. "I find it a little disturbing."

"That's good."

Her fingers unconsciously stroked the downy hair on Mark's head. "What do you mean?"

"I mean that if you didn't find all this," he waved a hand at the crowded, noisy room, "a little disturbing, I'd worry about you. It's what you do with what you feel that's important, though. I'll be assigning some kids to you, and you'll be responsible for working with them every day and going through their programs."

A slight frown creased Katie's brow. "Now I feel anxious. Wouldn't it be better for professionals to do that? I mean, take the children through their programs. That seems so important."

"It is. But you're perfectly capable of doing it." He sounded very firm and positive.

Katie wanted to ask what made him so sure. Instead she said, "How do you decide what to do? Are there guidelines, books that you follow?"

"Sure, there are books. But mostly we just spend time evaluating each child, giving him certain tests, watching him, gauging his responses, then we design a program to fit his specific needs. Here, I'll show you." He strode over to a desk that was tucked in a corner behind the cribs, and came back with a thick notebook. "We take the task-analysis approach—"

"Wait!" Katie held up her hands as if to ward off the flow of terms. "I'm not sure I should even be in this class."

He closed the notebook very carefully. "Miss Holland, yesterday I was a little irritated when I realized you had signed up because it was your only alternative."

"I noticed," she murmured.

"And now, you still aren't sure. That doesn't make me actually angry, but I'd certainly rather work with people who want to be here." He ran his fingers through his dark hair, then tried unsuccessfully to smooth it.

Katie thought he looked almost approachable ...almost. "Mr. Adams, I don't blame you for feeling that way. But could we give it until the end of the week, at least? Do you think you can stand having me around, indecisive as I am, for that long?" The words were light, and brightly spoken, but it hurt a little to have to beg. She did need the credits, but beyond that, for some reason she couldn't explain she wanted to come back here.

After a moment, during which he looked squarely and disconcertingly into her eyes, he nodded. "Fair enough." Then he moved away, a smile on his face as he saw one of the parents arrive. Katie thought it must be nearing the end of the session.

Partly because she wanted to ask him about Mark and partly because she wanted to help with the cleanup to erase the impression (however true) that all her reasons for signing up for this class were selfish, Katie found herself the last to leave. Cleanup after that bunch was no small chore.

Will showed no hint of his earlier irritation as he helped her into her coat and followed her out into the hall. She mustered the courage to ask, "How did you decide to go into this field, anyway?" He was silent as they walked to the outside door, making her think she'd asked the wrong question. "Look, if you'd rather not say, it's all right."

"No, it isn't that. I was just trying to think of how to tell you." His eyes had a distant, thoughtful look, and it wasn't until they were outside the building that he said,

"I suppose it all started when my nephew Tommy was born. He was my sister's second child, and the first grandson on both sides of the family."

Stoically Katie noticed the steady, fine mist that was falling—and realized she had no umbrella today. Aloud she said, "You must have all been thrilled."

Soberly he glanced at her. "As a matter of fact, none of us could talk about Tommy, or even think about him for weeks without choking up." His words conveyed a certain sadness, a deep feeling of sorrow.

"But why?" she asked, then wondered if she was prying or being discourteous. His silence reinforced that thought as they stood for a moment outside the door and Katie felt she should have just listened and let him talk.

As they walked slowly down the tree-lined street he seemed oblivious to the rain. Katie was on the verge of saying something polite and leaving. Then he said, "Tommy was born with Down's syndrome. I still think sometimes how shocked and sad everyone in the family was, and how that upset me."

Hesitantly, because she could see that although the pain was not new it was still very real, Katie said, "But wasn't it normal for everyone to feel sad and shocked that the baby had problems?"

He stopped walking for a moment and turned to face her. "You're right, of course. But all I could think of then was the contrast—how happy everyone was when Lisa, their older child, was born. From the beginning Lisa was an exceptional child. Not only was she beautiful, she rolled over early, walked at barely eight months, and could talk your arm off at fourteen months. Bright as a new penny, beautiful...an absolute joy of a little girl." He drew a deep breath, exhaled slowly. "I guess what I really felt was that Tommy deserved joy at his birth, too, and instead all of us were stunned and sad. It wasn't until later that we began to see how wonderful he is too, how fine..."

His words trailed off, and Katie thought perhaps he was embarrassed because of the love in them. She didn't feel embarrassed at all, just enormously touched. "Was it then that you decided to be a teacher?" she asked gently.

"I was already a teacher then."

Something had been in the back of Katie's mind all morning, since the first time she'd seen Will with Mark. "Have you always taught children this young?"

"No, why do you ask?"

Katie stuck her hands in her pockets, trying to think of how to phrase her thought, then said simply, "Because I've never seen a man teaching babies and little ones as you do."

His eyes narrowed but there was a smile lurking in the corners of them. "I suppose you think it's more fitting for a woman to do it?"

"No, I hadn't gone that far. I just hadn't seen a man in that role."

"Are you one of those hidebound traditionalists, Miss Holland?"

"I'm called Katie," she said, ignoring the edge in his voice. He seemed touchy about certain things. "And I don't know if I am or not." She hesitated a moment, then said, "No, I don't think so, if it means thinking men do this and women that and not crossing the lines."

"Then what are you?"

His question was so direct, so free of anything but an obvious desire to know that she found herself bound to answer honestly. "I...I guess I'm a woman who's not sure of anything as far as roles go except for my own need to find a place where I fit, where I belong and can be whatever is in me to be." She smiled ruefully. "I can't believe I just said that. It sounded so childish."

His gaze down at her was different now, almost as though he hadn't really looked at her before. "You don't have any illusions about yourself, do you?"

"No, should I?" Katie wasn't used to this sort of exchange. She and Justin talked mostly of his work, the food at whatever restaurant they were dining, even the weather, but not these kinds of things.

"I didn't mean you should, only that most people do," he responded easily. "I find it refreshing that you don't."

She was at a loss for words at that pronouncement, so she murmured, "I take it that you aren't a hidebound traditionalist."

His quick, deep laughter was pleasant. "In no way! I even have the effrontery to think there are a lot of things women do that I can do just as well." His grin was mischievous now. "However, I try to be fair, and have no prejudice whatever against women doctors, or jackhammer operators, or pilots, or whatever you might choose to be."

"There are certainly those who disagree," said Katie. "And you'll have to admit women might be just as upset as men if we invade traditional male territory. It gets confusing, you know, if all the lines cross and blur."

"That's true, and I don't want to tamper with God's design for men and women. There are differences, and I hope I always respect them," he said seriously.

Katie wanted to put a word in about being glad for those differences between men and women, but decided she didn't know him that well. "Are you saying that we can and should share in more roles, that for one reason or another have been strictly male or female up until now?" When he nodded she couldn't resist saying, "Then you could change a messy diaper and not feel your masculinity was threatened?"

"I've done it so many times now it would certainly take more than a messy diaper to threaten my masculinity."

His words were so calm and matter-of-fact Katie was impressed. This was no idle macho brag. She stole a peek at his strong profile and believed every word he spoke. He was a real man and would be in any woman's book—but different with a capital D. "I suppose that attitude helps you define yourself as a teacher of very young children, especially the babies."

"Yes, because you won't find many men in teaching positions like mine yet. I hope there will be more of us though, as people keep changing their attitudes."

"I can see where a man would have an advantage in a classroom," she said thoughtfully.

"The truth is, children need both men and women. I can talk until I'm blue in the face about men being able to fill a traditionally female role, but there's something about a woman's special kind of compassion, a woman's touch, that—" He stopped, then said, "I do tend to run on."

"And it's fascinating," said Katie softly. "Were you always in special education?"

"No, for three years I taught high school history." A wry smile twitched his mouth. "I understood where you were coming from when you said you had discipline problems."

"Really?" she murmured, wondering why that small confession pleased her so much. She shoved aside the thought that she probably looked like a drowned rat by now. The rain was steady, if not heavy.

"Really. I loved history—still do. But I never quite got the hang of making it interesting to thirty seventeen-year-olds, twenty-eight of whom think history is irrelevant. I struggled just to make it through those fifty-minute classes. Maybe if I'd worked harder on my presentations, or stuck with it longer, I'd have found a way to interest them, but I doubt it."

"So you were at the point of disillusionment with teaching, then?"

"I don't like to admit that. It sounds so trite." He smiled, his blue eyes meeting hers. "I'd rather believe it was just a step toward finding out what God really had in mind for my life."

"Oh, I see," said Katie. That he was a man who wanted to find out God's plan for himself was interesting; that he could talk about it openly and easily with no hint whatsoever of self-consciousness was even more interesting. And she caught another glimpse of his burning intensity. It seemed so strong Katie thought he might glow in the dark. "How old is your nephew now?"

"He's seven, and I think if he keeps on doing as well as he has been, he'll go to public school next year."

"I gather from your tone that's unusual for a Down's syndrome child."

"Yes, it is, but I believe absolutely that they could all do better if someone just cared enough to try harder to teach them, to stimulate them, to *make* them learn!" He stopped, realizing that a couple of girls passing by were staring at him, whispering under their umbrella. "Sorry. As I said before, I tend to get a little carried away," he said sheepishly. Then, surprised, he said, "Your hair is all wet! It's raining. We've been walking in the rain—"

"I know." Katie gave a wan smile.

He took her arm and steered her inside the student union building. "The least I can do is buy you a cup of coffee while you dry out."

"That sounds good," she said, hoping he'd go on about his nephew, not wanting to bring the subject up again, but knowing she was more than a little interested.

She needn't have worried. At a table in the corner of the coffee shop she spent the next hour not saying much beyond an occasional question and listening to the rambling, but never dull, account of how Will Adams arrived at the point where children like his nephew became the most important thing in his life. Katie, elbows on the table, chin on her hands, said, "I really envy your enthusiasm, your sense of knowing exactly what you want to do with your life."

His hands cradled the empty coffee mug as he looked

at her. "You sound as though that's something you're trying to decide."

"That's an understatement. I'm tired of trying first one thing, then another. It's uncomfortable, or worse, to be so uncommitted."

He nodded, a thoughtful look in his eyes as he gazed at her. "And I didn't make it any better by telling you not to join the ranks of bad teachers, did I?"

Katie shrugged, and said, "No, you didn't. You were right, of course, but if I don't find something that suits my peculiar talents pretty soon I'm going to die on the vine!"

Katie had very expressive brows. They were a shade darker than her hair, and right now they gave her face a tragicomic look that tempted Will Adams to chuckle. "Did you know your face talks even when you don't? You ought to be an actress."

Katie couldn't help bursting out laughing. "You've got to be joking! I'm not good-looking enough to be an actress."

That she was the kind of young woman who harbored no false modesty was obvious even to someone who'd known her as short a time as Will Adams had. He smiled as he said, "Oh, you're good-looking enough. And you've got something else, too."

Katie wasn't embarrassed by his words. On the contrary, they pleased her very much. It was the way he said them that unsettled her. She'd never met anyone like him before, and it was difficult to sort out the jumble of impressions crowding her mind at that moment. She was grateful when his mood suddenly changed and he said, "I don't know about you, but I'm hungry enough to eat the bark off a tree."

"Order a hamburger here and it won't be a whole lot different," Katie said pertly.

He smiled again and looked around for a waitress. To Katie's chagrin she saw that while they'd spent the last hour almost oblivious to the come-and-go crowd around them, the shift had changed and Sharon, who worked here in the coffee shop afternoons, was watching them from near the door.

In response to Will's smile, she came bustling over. "Yes, can I help you?"

Katie couldn't help but smile at the avid curiosity on Sharon's face. "Sharon, this is Will Adams." To Will she said, "Sharon is my roommate, and my friend, too, thank goodness."

"Glad to meet you, Sharon," Will said as he extended his hand. "We thought we'd try a hamburger—"

Sharon's expression and words cut him off. "Then you must be new on campus. Let me recommend the soup. It comes in a can." She gave that gap-toothed grin, and Katie could see Will responding to her warmth. "Like my grandpa used to say, this is the kind of joint where you oughta eat only a hard-boiled egg or a coconut."

Will laughed. "Soup it is. Is that all right with you?" he asked Katie.

She nodded, and when Sharon left, still throwing Will quick little curious looks, Katie thought how different this meal was from the one with Justin the night before. She also wondered how chicken noodle soup and crackers in cellophane seemed somehow every bit as good as what Le Bistro offered.

As they finished Will leaned forward over the small mountain of crinkly wrappers before him and said, "Sharon had a funny look on her face when you introduced me. I wonder why?"

She certainly wasn't going to tell him that Sharon had most likely been thinking it was about time Katie found someone besides Justin Moore, and was trying to decide if she approved of Will. Katie murmured something about Sharon's being a different sort of girl but a good friend, and he let it go.

That evening as Katie was plowing her way through a rather technical book on Down's syndrome, Sharon burst into the apartment. "Well, tell me all about him!" she sang out, shedding her shoes beneath the coffee table and her coat over the couch just before she flung herself onto it. "He's gorgeous. Where did you meet him? Justin will turn blue. Or green—money green. Oh, it's about time you found someone else!"

"Sharon!" But Katie couldn't really be angry at Sharon. "He's my instructor in special ed, not a date."

"With him for an instructor that class has to be your favorite this term," said Sharon, rolling her eyes. "So tell me, how did your first day go? As bad as you expected?"

The look on Katie's face was thoughtful. "Not the way I expected at all. It was—" Katie stopped, at a loss as to how to describe her day's experiences.

"Good or bad?" prompted Sharon.

"I'm not sure simple words like that can do it. The problems most of those children have to live with are unbelievable, worse than I ever dreamed possible."

"What are you talking about?"

Katie looked up, having just realized that Sharon didn't know, any more than she had, that the preschool was for developmentally disabled children. When she explained, Sharon's eyes grew even bigger than usual.

"I don't know if I could handle that," said Sharon doubtfully. "How about you?"

"There's something about them that has already caught my interest. They have to struggle against terrific odds just to accomplish things we never even think about. I was watching Will teach Jasmine to eat—she's four and has cerebral palsy—and I had no idea—"

Katie recited incident after incident and Sharon listened as she always did, with all her mind and even all her body. She leaned forward, her eyes wide with interest, her shaggy head nodding encouragement. When Katie finally ran down, Sharon said, "I've never seen you this excited about a class, or anything, for that matter."

33

"For a very good reason," said Katie wryly. "I've certainly never been so interested in anything. I stopped by the library and checked out this book on Down's syndrome, which several of the children in the preschool were born with."

"So what's Down's syndrome?"

Katie grinned. "Hey, I just started, don't expect too much. The only thing I'm sure of so far is they're finding that with careful teaching at home and in school Down's kids can learn skills the experts never used to think possible."

"You're caught. I can see it in your eyes, roomie."

"You may be right, Sharon," she said softly. "Did you know that the older a woman gets, the more likely she is to have a child with Down's syndrome?"

"Wow." Sharon hugged herself. "We'd better get started having babies right away, especially you. You're two years older than me!"

Katie's laughter rang out. "Don't you think I'd better find a husband first?"

"Well if you really get desperate, there's always Computer Man. But I can think of at least one alternative."

"Which is?" asked Katie, feeling she shouldn't have.

"How about that fine specimen you were with this afternoon?"

"Sharon! You always make something out of nothing."

Sharon nodded sagely. "Look, I'm the one who watched you talking for three-quarters of an hour, sweetie. For all either of you knew, the room could have been empty, until he got hungry. Is he married?" She always took the direct approach.

"Why, I don't know," Katie said faintly, wondering at the silly, sudden hope that he wasn't. Then another feeling stole over her, the quiet assurance that Will Adams would have, in the space of time they were together, mentioned a wife. He was that kind of man.

Chapter Three

On Thursday afternoon Justin called Katie from his office, saying that he was bringing dinner for the two of them and he wanted Katie to wear the cheong sam he'd bought for her on his last business trip to Hong Kong. Katie was bright enough to translate these little bits of information. When Sharon got home from work she walked into a softly lit livingroom, the low coffee table carefully set with the antique china Sharon's grandmother had given her and several cushions on the floor around it.

"I hope you don't mind my using your china without asking," said Katie, as she stood in the kitchen doorway and surveyed her handiwork. A nosegay of violets nestled between two once tall candles which had obligingly burned to a fairly even height. She planned to light them when Justin knocked so they'd look new. She sighed. It wasn't always easy to keep up with Justin—or to be more fair, with what she felt Justin expected.

"Hey, that looks terrific. Of course I don't mind. But are you entertaining a midget? I know I said you ought to branch out and date new people, but this is ridiculous." She started to discard her shoes, caught a glimpse of the warning on Katie's face, and took her things to the bedroom. She yelled from there, "Is it that good-

35

looking instructor, I hope?"

"No," Katie called back, looking quickly in the mirror to see if her piled-high hair was still in its rather elaborate fluff of curls. It was. Even Katie had to admit it looked all right, with only a few straying wisps around her face and neck. She smoothed the golden silk of the beautiful dress. It did fit well, as Justin said admiringly every time he persuaded her to wear it. The high mandarin neck was very flattering, and she'd learned to minimize her movements so that the almost thigh-high slit in the side wasn't *too* obvious. "Justin's bringing Chinese food."

"Justin? But Katie-love, I'd hoped..." Sharon came out of the bedroom in jeans and a sweatshirt with her running shoes in hand. She dropped to the floor, muttering to herself as she jammed her feet into them.

"What did you say, Sharon?"

She looked up. "I said I was willing to spend the evening at the library even though I don't need to so you could...oh, get better acquainted with this Will Adams. But now I *know* I'll spend the evening at the library. Computer Man would choke on his egg foo yung if I hang around."

"You don't have to leave," said Katie quietly. She loved Sharon and trusted her judgment even if she did act a little zany at times. And it troubled Katie more than she cared to admit that Sharon had never liked Justin.

"Oh, yes I do. See you later, roomie."

Like a tiny whirlwind she was gone, leaving Katie at the window, watching the dusk softly cover the pale green beginnings on the trees. One reason she loved this apartment was the high, lofty view of trees, sky, and rooftops, and the general feeling of space. She often stood and stared dreamily out the wide window with its small panes. When she saw Justin drive up and easily slip his four-door sedan into a spot that would have made her break out in hives, she sighed. He could probably mentally compute the distance he needed to park in centimeters.

She hurried to light the candles before he came up the stairs and was able to open the door before he rang the bell. "Come in," she said, a little breathless, and not at all aware of the picture she made. The candlelight behind her outlined her tall, slim, golden figure and the soft shimmer of her hair.

Justin stood quite still for a long moment, then said, his voice low, "Kathleen, I'm sure you must be the most beautiful sight in the world."

As she stood aside she found a smile, but no words. Justin often made her feel as though there was nothing she could say to match his extravagant statements. Finally she murmured, "I hope you don't think I've overdone it."

He had caught sight of the carefully set table, the cushions on the floor. "No, not at all. That's a delightful idea. I admire a person who has imagination and ingenuity." He took the large bag he carried to the kitchen and came immediately back to her, purpose plain in his eyes.

But Katie kissed him quickly on his smooth-shaven cheek, then slipped away. "I'd better set dinner out, or it will get cold. Did you bring fried won ton?"

An amused smile played about his mouth as he nodded. "Your favorite? Of course I did. And egg foo yung, shrimp, chicken sub gum, pork-fried rice, and—"

"Stop, let's eat before I starve to death!" Katie laughed and began to arrange food on platters and bowls as Justin leaned against the door frame, watching her with that disturbing look still in his eyes.

Dinner was fun. Katie had to admit Justin could be very entertaining as he told her of the latest shakeup in his company. As usual, he'd come out well, a step higher on the corporate ladder. As she surveyed their empty plates which had been heaped full at the beginning of the meal, Katie said slowly, "You may be president of that company someday, the way you're going."

His gray eyes looked directly, steadily at her. "Not may be—will be. Count on it. I decided a long time ago what my goals are, and being at the top is one of them. I have another goal, Kathleen."

Katie bit her lip, then reached for the teapot instead of asking what he meant. "More tea? We haven't eaten our fortune cookies yet. I always like to have them with tea—"

"Let me read yours," he said, reaching for the cookie, closing his hand over Katie's for a moment. He broke the crisp wafer in half, pulled out the sliver of paper and read slowly, "You will say *yes* very soon to a very important proposal—"

Wide-eyed, Katie asked, "Does it really say that?" She stuck out her hand and Justin, chuckling, watched as Katie scanned the brief message and burst out laughing. "Oh, you, this says *be careful of your investments*!"

"That, too."

They were still laughing when Sharon breezed in, saying carelessly, "Justin, I thought you'd be gone."

Katie knew very well Sharon didn't think Justin would be gone. It was only half past eight and his car was parked in full view outside. But in a strange way Katie wasn't the least bit aggravated; she was even vaguely relieved.

Justin hid his own irritation well, but Katie knew it was there. When he rose from the cushion he said, "I really should be getting home."

"Hey, don't let me chase you off. It's early." Sharon plunked herself down cross-legged on the couch.

"I have an eight o'clock conference in the morning," he said with a smile that didn't fool anyone, least of all Sharon. "Have you eaten? There's certainly plenty left if you like cold Chinese food." The way he said it, cold Chinese food fell in the same category as chocolate-covered bumblebees.

"Are you kidding?" Sharon grinned. "It's right up

there on my list, close to cold pizza."

Justin couldn't entirely hide the grimace of distaste on his face. "Walk me to the car, Kathleen?"

"Sure. Be right back, Sharon."

"Now that's a good idea," muttered Sharon. "*Right* back."

Katie closed the door quickly behind her, glancing at Justin and wondering if he'd heard. His words as they walked down the stairs made her suspect that he had. And yet, even if he hadn't she knew he was sensitive enough to pick up the vibrations in the very air around Sharon, who was as transparent as a clean windowpane.

"I don't think she likes me."

"Oh, Justin, that's not so!" protested Katie a little more strongly than she should have.

"Maybe it's not that she dislikes me, she just doesn't think I'm right for you."

Katie was honest enough not to deny that. "Justin, I—"

As they went out onto the wide veranda he stopped and gathered her close. "But she's wrong, Katie, she's wrong. There's no one else in the world for me. You're the one I want, the one God wants for me. He told me so."

His lips were warm against her forehead, his arms tight around her. Katie couldn't speak, and she knew if he kissed her she wouldn't pull away. He was so sure, so strong and dependable, and—

A gust of rainy spring wind whipped around the corner, making Katie gasp. Justin's kiss was quick and warm. "You go on back up. It's cold out here, and I don't want you getting sick. We've got plans to make, Kathleen, and I want you to be thinking very seriously about answering that question in your fortune cookie. You know what I'm talking about." He started down the steps, then called back, "I meant to ask, what time do you finish your classes tomorrow?"

"I was going to the preschool to look over some of the children's data sheets at 4:30, after my last class."

"Good, I'll pick you up then. There's a party I'd like you to attend with me tomorrow evening and some important people I want you to meet."

Before she could answer he turned to go, and Katie heard him say softly, "I love you." She stood in the drafty doorway for a long while after he drove away.

Inside, Sharon was blissfully devouring the last of the shrimp when Katie came slowly in, a thoughtful look on her face. "What's wrong, roomie?"

"Nothing's wrong, not really. Justin wants me to go to a party tomorrow evening."

"And you hate parties," put in Sharon. "But there's something else, isn't there?" She had a fat shrimp poised in mid-air, the forefinger of her hand pointed straight at Katie.

She smiled. "You know me pretty well."

"Better than our friend Computer Man, it seems. Come on, out with it."

Katie sank onto the other end of the sofa. "He says God told him that I'm the right one for him." She sighed a little, bracing herself for Sharon's probably caustic retort.

But Sharon's reply was very gentle and perceptive. "Maybe so, Katie. But if you are, God will tell you, too. It'll be so loud and clear in your own heart you'll think he's on a P.A. system. Don't worry."

Katie smiled. She had been a Christian for five years, Sharon only two. But once again Katie realized that Sharon's grasp of spiritual truth far exceeded hers in some matters. "I love you a lot, you fruitcake. Now finish your shrimp, and there's more won ton in the kitchen." Somehow she felt much, much better. She knew Sharon was right.

The next afternoon at the preschool she was pleased to be asked to sit in on a conference between Mark's mother and Will. As he'd explained, parent training was a vital part of their program, and besides, little Mark already had a special spot in her heart. She sat on the opposite side of the playroom leafing through some of the other children's notebooks and listened carefully as Will talked with Lila Evans, who held Mark in her lap.

Will was saying earnestly, "Your participation is very important. In fact, you carry the major responsibility for teaching Mark."

The slender blonde woman's face showed quick concern. "But I thought that was the reason for bringing him here to school...so young." She dropped a featherlight kiss on the baby's head. "It's hard leaving him."

"And a bit of a relief as well not to have the whole burden on you?" asked Will gently, knowing it wasn't an easy question to answer.

Lila Evans met his eyes. "Yes, I guess it is. It's just that he's so little, so young to be away from us all morning long."

"That's true. But you can help select his goals. You can collect information on his progress for us and be as much his teacher as I am."

A smile lightened the young mother's face. "That sounds pretty good."

"It is. You'll be a real partner in helping Mark reach his fullest potential." He reached out and stroked Mark's chin, then held out his arms. The baby went readily to him, and after he cuddled him a moment Will said to Katie, "Would you like to hold tiger here while I go over his program with Mrs. Evans?"

"I'd love to," said Katie, putting down the notebook and coming over to take the baby. Mark grinned shyly at her, making her certain he remembered her.

The next three-quarters of an hour flew by for Katie. When she saw Justin at the door, she realized with dismay that it was almost an hour past the time she said she'd meet him.

He stood for a moment, looking around the room,

then came over to her. "I've been waiting outside for you since 4:30." He looked at his watch, and Katie bit her lip as she looked at her own. 5:20.

"Oh, Justin, I'm sorry! I lost track of the time. Mark and I have been reading and playing with the blocks." It didn't sound like much of an excuse even to Katie. Out of the corner of her eye she could see that Lila Evans and Will had finished and were standing up.

Justin's eyes were on Mark and the expression on his handsome face was indecipherable as he said flatly, "I see."

Katie thought he was about to say something more and when he didn't she asked, "Would you like to hold him?" She held out a willing Mark and missed the look on Justin's face. But Will, who had moved closer, didn't. He also took in the smartly tailored suit, the correct tie and perfectly groomed hair.

"Here, I'll take Mark," he offered. "My name is Will Adams, and you are—"

The abruptness in his tone puzzled Katie as she said, "Mr. Adams, this is my...friend, Justin Moore."

"How do you do?" murmured Justin politely as he put an arm casually around Katie's shoulders and drew her slightly closer to him. Much the same as Will had earlier assessed him, Justin's calm gray eyes surveyed the other man's jeans, the open-necked gingham shirt, the well-used track shoes.

"Very well, thank you," was the crisp reply from Will. He rubbed Mark's back gently, almost as though he was not aware of doing it.

Katie felt something in the air, but before she could analyze it Justin said to her, "I can see you aren't yet through. Sorry to have barged in. I'll wait for you outside. Nice to have met you." His smile and nod at Will were perfunctory, polite; the last fleeting look at Mark unreadable. All three of them, including Mark's mother, watched as he strode from the room.

The oddly tense silence that followed was broken by

Mark's "Ma ma, ma ma," as Lila took him from Will. "Thank you so much for going over the program with me," she said.

Will's answer was absentminded, though he gathered up several books and pamphlets and gave them to her before she left. Then he came back and stood for a moment in front of the window, his back to Katie as he stared out at the dying afternoon. The lovely, special green of early spring seemed to color even the air outside. The rain had cleared and everything looked ready to burst into life.

"Well," said Katie uncertainly, "I'd better go."

"Yes, your friend is waiting." He turned suddenly, and his face was serious. "Mark made him acutely uncomfortable."

"I...what do you mean?"

"Some people are simply unable to accept children like Mark."

"Oh, I don't think Justin felt—" She stopped, for she didn't know exactly how to go on.

"It makes me angry."

The tense words were low and vehement, and Katie frowned. "You don't know that's what Justin felt."

"Believe me, I know. It's not the first time I've seen that look."

"I think you're being..." Katie didn't finish that sentence, either. She'd been about to say judgmental, but the word wouldn't come out. "I'd better go. I'll see you on Monday."

"Are you sure you want to come back?" His eyes challenged her, made her feel defensive again.

"Haven't I done all right this week?"

He backed down a little at her defiant question. They both knew she'd done very well indeed. "Ah...yes, you have. I've been watching you closely."

Katie swallowed, wondering why those quiet words made her suddenly feel as though she needed to get outside, where there was more air. "I'll be here Monday,

43

and don't worry, Mr. Adams, I'll do my share."

He looked as though he were fighting it, but a tiny smile won the battle. "Good. I'll expect it." As she went out the door, she heard him call out, "Call me Will, I'm not *that* much older than you are!"

When Katie slipped into the car Justin smiled, too, but it seemed forced. Instead of asking what was on his mind, she said, "I'm sorry to have made you wait, Justin. It won't take me long to get ready for the party."

"That's good. The Andersons are very important people."

His tone was polite, not accusatory. But she felt the implication that they were late and it was her fault. "I thought I'd wear the blue dress you gave me last Christmas." A sudden realization hit her. Whenever she was with Justin she tended—no, she made it a point to wear something he'd given her, or picked out for her. She never trusted her own taste, her own judgment about clothes.

It was an interesting insight that she didn't have time to explore, for Justin was saying, "I'd like that. You look lovely in it, Kathleen." He braked the car in front of her apartment. "I'll wait for you here in the car."

"But Justin, you're welcome to come in, you know that."

He shook his head. "I have plenty to keep me busy." He reached for his briefcase in the back seat with one hand and waved her out with the other, managing to glance at his watch in the process. Justin had a way of doing three things at once with perfect coordination that intimidated Katie.

She smiled and got out of the car, but as she took the stairs two at a time, her mind was racing too. *He probably didn't want to see Sharon again. He probably stayed in the car to save time…to show me without words I made him late and…*Katie gave up trying to decipher Justin's actions. She breezed through the livingroom with a superficially gay explanation about

44

the party to Sharon, and went straight to her closet to examine the blue dress.

She breathed a sigh of relief. No spots. It was a sad fact of life that more often than not Katie dropped a bit of this or that, and she was grateful her mother had taught her to get almost anything out of almost anything. As she quickly scrubbed her face with cleansing cream and brushed her teeth, Katie thought with sudden longing of her mother. It had been almost a month since she'd been home to visit.

Moisturizer, a light foundation, blush, just a bit of coppery brown shadow, mascara, lip gloss in soft rose, and she was through. She brushed her hair back, glad it hadn't been rained on all day, found her coat, and barely gave Sharon a chance to comment on how she looked.

"Tell Computer Man I missed seeing him," were the last words Sharon called out.

"And bite your tongue for lying," muttered Katie as she hurried down the stairs.

Justin, who'd seen her coming, was out of the car and waiting with the door open before she reached it. Once inside and on the way she took a deep breath that ended in a sigh, her eyes closed. *You're going to a party, Katie, you're with a handsome man, you're going to have a good time.* Somehow she wanted to repeat to herself the advice she'd muttered to Sharon—bite your tongue.

The Andersons lived in a very exclusive neighborhood in an imposing home. Katie wasn't at all surprised when a woman in a black dress, white lacy cap and apron to match answered the door. As they entered the discreetly lit, thirty-four-foot livingroom—obviously "decorator done" in plums and burgundies and mauves, in glass and brass—several people descended on them. For the next hour she did what she always did at parties if she could manage to get away with it. She sat quietly in an out-of-the-way corner with a glass of ginger ale in her hand while Justin made the circuit. Justin could talk to anyone, and about an amazing variety of subjects.

She watched him, his shining blond head bent attentively to a chic, dark-haired young woman who had monopolized him for almost fifteen minutes. Justin was going to do exactly as he said—go right to the top. And men with his drive and determination were always irresistible to women. The woman who married Justin Moore would have to accept that fact.

The noise level of the room was fairly high, but for a moment it faded completely away as Katie suddenly tried to imagine herself as Justin's wife. He had been slowly moving toward her, the dark-haired young woman drifting with him. The image of herself as Mrs. Justin Moore didn't fully materialize before it dissipated altogether in the flurry of introductions.

The dark-haired woman, who was a computer analysis expert, was joined by two other young women and a clone of Justin—except that he had brown hair and glittering blue eyes. The clothes and the intent, alert look in their eyes were the same—that avid, eager air of *let's conquer the world,* written indelibly on their faces. Katie managed to murmur the correct, bright, interested replies, and later not to spill Trout Amandine on her lap during dinner.

In the car going home she leaned her head wearily against the seat.

"Have a good time?" asked Justin.

"What? Oh, yes, of course. It was a very nice party, and the house was beautiful."

"Yes," he enthused, "I know the decorator they hired. He's great. And Bibi Anderson has it down to a science—dinner parties, I mean. There were quite a few important people there, some of whom, for very good reasons, could have been at each other's throats. She saw to it that they weren't, though. Yes, I'd say Bibi is a real asset to her husband. She served a perfect dinner and managed to circulate so that no one knifed anyone in the back." He glanced over at her in the dimness. "And that's no mean feat."

"The dinner was very good," agreed Katie faintly.

"Yes," said Justin. "The right wife is very important to a man."

"I'm sure that's true—" Katie halted, the noise of the crowded room they'd just left still ringing in her ears. She didn't want to talk about the party, or perfect company wives any longer.

"What did you think of the preschool?" she asked suddenly.

He was silent for a moment as he slowed to a stop and signaled to turn off the freeway. "It looked like an adequate setup," was his cautious comment. No mention at all of Mark, or anything that might refute Will's supposition that the baby had disturbed him.

After a moment's hesitation Katie decided against pressing for his reaction to Mark, but something prompted her to say, "And Will?"

"He seemed nice enough." There it was again, the caution in his tone.

"Just nice? You didn't get any other impressions?" Rather recklessly Katie added, "I think Will Adams would call for a stronger reaction from most people. I find him awfully...intense."

"That's probably true," he said slowly, as though he were trying to make up his mind whether or not to say more. "But I also sensed an arrogance in the man that bothered me."

"Arrogance?" echoed Katie, frowning. *Arrogance?* She would have to think about it, but there was a distinct possibility that Justin was right.

"Yes, as well as the fact that he's attracted to you."

The quiet words fell like a bomb into Katie's mind. "To me? Why, Justin, you're imagining things! I've never known you to be jealous—"

"I didn't say I was jealous," Justin interrupted calmly.

"Jealousy is a wasteful, destructive emotion."

Katie nodded, and because he was quiet for the rest of the ride to her apartment, she was too.

When he left her at her door, the warmth of his lips still lingering on her own, she was relieved to see Sharon's bedroom door closed and no light beneath. Sometimes Sharon used up all that marvelous energy and went to bed early.

Katie's own room was a shambles after her frantic rush to get ready. She undressed slowly, put on her robe, then went about setting things right again. It was a homey, comfortable room done mostly in blue and beige, with small touches of rose and cream here and there. The quilt on her bed, a combination of all four colors, had been her mother's first attempt. She'd often told Katie how many mistakes there were in it, that she should never have chosen such a difficult pattern.

She stood in the center of the room and let her eyes wander from the lovely Storm-at-Sea design of the hand-stitched quilt and lace pillow shams, to the dusky-blue velvet chair, the old lace curtains at the windowed bay, and to the antique rose and amber Tiffany lamp which had been a sacrificial gift from her mother.

Katie had arranged and rearranged her beloved collection of sea pictures until she thought they looked just right on the one solid wall opposite the bed. There was a Dalhart Windberg print of sand dunes off Padre Island, south of the Texas coast, two small original oils by a beginning artist in Manzanita, three wonderfully wild photographs of the Oregon coast during storms, and a huge framed collage of all the beautiful bits of driftwood she'd collected on the beach, their silvery beiges and grays soothing to the eyes. The room was such a pleasant one she didn't mind cleaning it.

But she finally admitted to her consciousness the things she'd been putting off thinking about—her deep emotional reaction to the children at the school, and, she might as well admit, to Will Adams—not to mention the evening she'd spent with Justin.

She ran hot water into the deep, old-fashioned, clawfoot, iron bathtub, added lavender bath oil, and lowered her body into the steaming fragrance. Even as a little girl she had maintained warm water helped her to think as well as soaking her clean. But not this time. The water grew cold, and, shivering, she scrambled out and dried off, still puzzling over the fact that her life seemed on the verge of splitting neatly into two separate parts.

Her conversation with God that night was not clear, but she knew as she drifted off to sleep that He would guide her heart and mind even if she wasn't sure of what lay ahead herself.

Chapter Four

Katie had an early class on Monday and didn't arrive at the preschool until after nine o'clock. Will seemed preoccupied, and told her she could observe him with Eddie, one of the children he'd decided to assign to her. She watched carefully as he guided Eddie through his program. The boy's bright eyes were glued to Will's face as he valiantly struggled with the first task, rainbow rings on a graduated peg.

"No, Eddie, red first, then orange, or the others won't fit." The next exercise was speech therapy. Katie had to work hard not to smile as Will said, his mouth pursed tightly, "Moo, Eddie, the cow says moooo."

"Very good cow, Mr. Adams," murmured Katie solemnly.

He looked up, a surprised expression on his face as though he'd forgotten she was there. "Would you finish Eddie's speech therapy, now that you've seen how it goes?" He rose from his chair and handed her Eddie's notebook.

With only a moment's hesitation she slipped into his chair. It was harder than she thought it would be, but she and Eddie made it to the end of his program, with Eddie cooperating beautifully. Katie felt Will's hand on her shoulder briefly as he said, "That's good for the first time. You do a pretty mean turkey, Miss Holland."

She glanced up into his eyes, absurdly pleased at the gently teasing praise. "I'll get better, won't I?"

He nodded, a thoughtful expression on his face now. "There's no doubt of that." Then he moved to corner Julie, swooping her up into his arms. The two of them were soon engrossed in her program, leaving Katie with Eddie. He beamed up at her, then darted away. She started to call him back, but saw that he was rummaging through the books. In a moment he gave a happy shout and came racing back, *Pooh* in hand. She spent the next half hour on the floor with Eddie nestled in her lap, his deep, funny little belly chuckles delighting her until she glanced at her watch.

"Uh, oh, Eddie, I'll be late for class if I don't leave now." He took the curtailment of Pooh's woozle hunt philosophically and even gave Katie a sweet smack of good-bye on her cheek. Because Will was still involved, she didn't say anything to him, just slipped out.

It was difficult to concentrate on Social Science for Elementary Teachers. Katie found herself wishing, and not for the first time, that all she had to do was work in the preschool. When her classes were finally over, she returned for her car, which she'd left parked at the rear of the education building. But to her dismay it wouldn't start. Just as though she knew what to look for, she opened the hood of the ancient little Subaru and peered in.

"Got a problem?"

She glanced up to see Will Adams peering over her shoulder, a stack of papers and folders in his hands. "Oh, am I glad to see you! This car won't start."

"What if I told you I wasn't mechanically inclined in the least? Would you still be glad to see me?"

Katie heard the teasing note in his voice and hesitated before she answered him. "As a matter of fact, I would. Then I'd say, that makes two of us who are not mechanically inclined, and I would ask who you call when your car quits."

He laid the stack of papers on top of the car and leaned over the engine. "The truth is, I'm a pretty fair shade-tree mechanic. Hmmmm." He fiddled with a wire here and there, twisted a cap or something—the things mechanics always did with immediate results.

"I suppose I should take that course I've heard about—the one where they teach women basic auto maintenance," she murmured.

He nodded. "Yes, you should. See if it'll start now."

She did as she was told. Sure enough, the contrary motor cranked immediately. As he gathered up his papers she said, "I really appreciate this. My mother's expecting me to come home this afternoon, and you know how mothers are. I'm almost twenty-five years old, but if I'm a half hour late she worries."

The car window was down and he bent over, his arms resting there, his face close to hers. "Where does your mother live?"

His eyes are very blue, Katie mused. *Not gray blue ...just...* She smiled in spite of herself as she thought, *True Blue.*

"What are you smiling about?"

She replied hastily, "The answer to your first question is Lincoln City over on the beach, and to the second...I was just thinking that you would like her."

"I don't doubt it. I like her daughter."

Although she had decided it wasn't a good idea to gaze into those true-blue eyes any longer, Katie couldn't keep from thinking what nice teeth he had; how firm looking and well shaped his mouth was. "I had the distinct impression that first day we met that you thought I was dangerous."

"You'll have to admit you were somewhat wild with that ridiculous yellow umbrella." For a moment he just looked at her, a steady, appraising look that she couldn't break away from. "And I'm not altogether sure you aren't more dangerous just sitting there, with no umbrella or weapon of any kind, except..."

"Except what?" she asked faintly.

There was a slight hesitation before he answered, "I'll tell you sometime," then looked at his watch. "I'm all through for the day. What would you say if I invited myself to go along with you? Think your mother would like me as much as you say I'll like her?"

Katie nodded, a curious mixture of pleasure and apprehension filling her. "But we'd better get going." She watched his easy, long strides carry him around the car, wondering why he'd asked to come. When they turned onto the coast highway, she phrased the question as casually as she could. "Why did you want to come, anyway?"

"Oh, there are a couple of reasons." He looked over at her, then said, "Tell me about Justin Moore."

Katie was taken aback for a second by his request, but she said slowly, "He works for an electronics firm based in Salem, and intends to be president of the company."

"Think he'll make it?"

"Yes, Justin is a determined man."

"I see. How long have you been dating?"

She had to think. It suddenly seemed like forever. Katie could barely remember going out with anyone else. "Almost two years, I believe."

"You're engaged, then?"

She saw the little frown dent between his eyes. "No, we're not engaged."

He lifted his brows in surprise, and the frown disappeared. "Is that because he hasn't asked you, or because he did and you said no?"

"You ask a lot of questions, Will Adams, and by the way, you haven't answered mine yet."

"I forgot what it was." His grin was catching.

"Why you wanted to come along with me today." Although she was cautiously enjoying the interchange between them, she felt safer asking questions than answering them.

"Two reasons. One is, I come from New Mexico and

have only been to the beach once."

"That's awful!" she exclaimed. "I spent my teen years on the coast, and have to go back every so often or I'll dry up and blow away. What's the other reason?"

Softly he said, "I find the more I'm around you, the more I want to be."

Katie watched the familiar landmarks slip by for a few miles before she trusted herself to speak again. "If you're from New Mexico you probably could use some good, damp Oregon coast air—but you'd better watch out, or you'll get web feet like the rest of us."

"I certainly don't have them now. I was born in Albuquerque, but my folks moved to Santa Fe not long after, and that's about as far away from webfoot country as you can get. Ever been there?" She shook her head and he went on enthusiastically, "It's beautiful, and has a fascinating history. You'd like it."

"I'm sure I would."

"Maybe someday I can show you the Santa Fe I knew as a kid growing up. As colorful as the regular tourist attractions are, the real heart of the city is off the beaten path. I suppose it's always that way." He put his arm on the back of the seat, his fingers just touching her shoulder. "Now, are you positive your mother won't mind my barging in?" He laughed. "It's a little late to be wondering about that, I guess, and you haven't mentioned your dad. Does he still have to pass judgment on the guys you bring home?"

"My father lives on the Oregon-Idaho border, and has ever since he divorced Mom," said Katie in a cold, brittle voice.

"I see." Will was quiet for a moment, then asked gently, "Is this a recent thing?"

"No, it happened ten years ago."

"That's a long time to be bitter, Katie."

She gave him a quick, almost angry glance. "What makes you think I'm bitter?"

"I can hear it in your voice."

His tone was so kind, so understanding that she felt the sting of tears. "You're mistaken. I don't care enough to be bitter."

"If you keep covering them up and pretending you don't have those feelings, they'll eat you alive."

"Look, when I was fourteen he came home one night and she was with him—"

"Who?"

"The girl who'd been working as his research assistant. My dad was forty, she was twenty. A blonde, blue-eyed Barbie doll," she finished harshly.

"Would you believe me if I told you he quit his high-powered, high-paying job so he could be a...a *river man*?" she asked, choking a little on the words. Will's quizzical frown spurred her on. "Run the rapids, live free—he lives on Pine Creek, not far from Hell's Canyon, and that's about as far from civilization, Mom and me as he can get." Disgustedly she added, "He's like a middle-aged Huck Finn."

"That must have been rough." His voice was gentle, but it didn't soothe her helpless anger.

"Are your parents still together?"

The quick question demanded an immediate reply, but he took his time answering. "They've had their share of problems and heartaches. I have a younger brother who's been in and out of trouble since he was twelve and it's caused them no end of—"

"But are they still together?" she persisted.

"Yes, but I'm trying to tell you it hasn't been easy, that it never is."

"I'm certainly well aware of that. However, you can't possibly understand what it's like having your parents divorce if you haven't been through it. Dad kept saying he was sorry, that he couldn't help himself, that he loved her...that she made him feel—" Katie choked, unable to continue.

He finished for her. "Like he was twenty, too." She

55

nodded numbly. "How did your mother make it through all this?"

"Mom's a survivor. She wasn't a Christian then, and she was mad clear through. He would have given her anything she asked for to get out of the marriage."

"What did she ask for?"

For the first time in quite a few miles Katie smiled. "The beach house. It's a marvelous old home with four bedrooms, three baths, a huge livingroom plus a sunroom, no less, and an attic big enough to accommodate a family of practicing Italian circus performers."

He laughed, obviously relieved to see her lighter mood. "What in the world did she want with a house that size?"

Katie looked at him as though he'd taken leave of his senses. "Look, besides being the neatest house you could imagine, *it's at the beach*!" she said, implying there couldn't possibly be two more compelling reasons to want a house. "And my mom is, in a homely way, quite possibly the best cook in the whole world."

"Now I know I'm glad I invited myself! But what does her cooking ability have to do with anything, except my gastronomic pleasure this evening, that is?"

"She was smart enough to know what she's best suited for, so she enrolled in the bed-and-breakfast program, and can have a full house practically any time she wants. Holland House is a popular place with people lucky enough to discover it. Not only that, she's developed a sideline, a sort of soup catering business."

"That sounds interesting, especially to a bachelor," said Will.

"And when you taste Mom's soup you'll find out why it's in demand," said Katie a little smugly. "She may never get rich, but she's not dependent on anyone." It was in her voice again, the bitterness.

"She must have been devastated by what your dad did, if she loved him," put in Will softly.

Katie nodded. "Mom will probably never marry

again. She keeps saying once was more than enough."

"Do you agree with her, Katie? How do you feel about marriage?"

After a moment of contemplating his question, Katie had to admit she couldn't answer it. Instead she said, "Sometimes I worry about Mom. But when I ask her if she's lonely, she always tells me she has more than enough to keep her busy."

"Busy people get lonely, too," Will said thoughtfully. "I can vouch for that."

"But you love your work with the kids, don't you?"

"It's deeply satisfying, even more than I ever thought it would be. In fact, I tend to lose myself in it, or so I've been told."

Katie wanted to ask who had told him, but couldn't bring herself to. It was probably some young woman who felt he wasn't spending enough time with her.

"We're almost there. Mom was expecting me at four, and it's half past."

"She wasn't expecting me, though. I don't imagine you often bring people home without asking her." When Katie shook her head he said casually, "Have you brought Justin to meet your mother?"

"Of course I have. Why do you ask so many questions?"

"Because I want to know the answers, why else?" he said easily, managing to ask yet another.

That stumped Katie, but she set her jaw, and he took it as a warning and didn't ask any more questions until they drove into Lincoln City. As she drove down the bumpy, familiar road toward home, she reveled in the sight of the ocean—*her* ocean. There was a storm brewing. She could see it in the foaming anger of the waves, almost feel the bite of the salty wind. "Oh, I can't wait to get out in it!"

"Would you like for me to drive while you get out and walk?" he asked drily, never dreaming she'd take him up on it.

Katie surprised him. "Would you?" She was already braking and pulling over to the side of the road. "Our house is on the end, the last one on the point."

"Your mother—"

But Katie was already out of the car, enjoying the look of surprise on his face. "Tell her I couldn't wait. She'll understand!" Then, feeling free, loving the smell of the sea and the sight of the wide, darkening sky, she ran down the worn path between two small, shuttered weekend houses. The people who owned them came so seldom that they had a forlorn air to them. As a girl Katie had created a life for the houses in her mind, and felt their loneliness along with her own after her father had left.

As she went from the loose, drier sand to that closer to the sea and firm with water, a gull wheeled above her head, calling out a greeting. She ran easily, swiftly at the water's edge, skirting the lacy scallops of foam, wishing she'd left the car sooner and had longer to run, because there *it* was—*the House*. Somehow, in her mind she always capitalized the word.

A well-proportioned white Cape Cod with tall red brick chimneys at either end, it had dormers piercing the weathered gray-shingle roof and darker gray shutters gracing the sides of the many-paned windows. It wasn't exactly built on a cliff. The grassy slope that led up to the House was far too gentle and civilized to fit the sinister image of mysterious old cliffside houses in the multitude of Gothic novels she'd once read. They had been her escape during those days when it had been as stormy inside the House as it sometimes was out. Her parents' divorce had not been one of the friendly ones she'd heard people on television discuss. Somehow the divorces of her friends' parents were never like that, either. She stopped, staring up at the House. It never failed to welcome her.

Now she could see Will's tall figure beside her mother, both of them waving to her as she scrambled up the rocky incline which bordered the lawn. The path was not as defined as it had been when Katie had lived here and used it daily.

"Katie!"

Loving the gladness in her mother's voice, Katie hurried toward her. Though she knew that it didn't happen often between mothers and daughters, Katie considered Marge Holland a friend, a good friend.

"Will has been assuring me it wasn't your fault you're late, Katie."

Katie hugged her tight. "I hope you weren't worried."

"No, not worried, just anxious to see you. It's been over a month since you've been here. I get so busy the days melt into each other, but when I checked the calendar, there it was."

Will was watching, an interested, thoughtful expression on his face. "I hope my being here won't be an inconvenience."

"Don't be silly," said Marge with a laugh. "There's always a pot of—"

"Soup on the stove," Katie finished for her. "What kind?"

"Clam chowder. Did you get enough walk?" Katie grinned at her mother and shook her head. "Then go on, and I'll set another place at the table. Will, are you cold? You can come on up to the house if you like. Katie would live in a driftwood shack on the sand and be a beach bum if I'd let her." She waited for him to answer, her slim angular body much like Katie's, her short, unobtrusively graying blonde hair ruffling in the stiff breeze.

Will glanced at Katie as he said, "If it's all right with your daughter I'd really enjoy a walk, too."

Marge laughed again, a nice hearty sound. "Then I'd better stir up some muffins, too. You'll be starving when you get back. Do you have a cap, Katie?"

Katie rolled her eyes, but drew a navy beret from her

pea-jacket pocket. "We won't be too long, Mom."

As Marge started toward the house the wind caught at her words. "I've heard that before!"

Will and Katie walked without talking for perhaps a mile. The mighty sound of the surf was conversation enough. Occasionally one of them spied a small offering from the sea: an amber nugget of agate, a Chinaman's Hat shell, a smooth lima bean-shaped rock. Finally Katie stopped, arms hugged tightly around her body, eyes staring out at the awesome expanse of sky and wind-whipped water.

Will ventured softly, "You really love it, don't you?"

She nodded. "When I'm confused, or tired, or...or hurt, I can come and walk on the beach—soak it all in, and God heals me. He's here, you know."

Will was quiet for a moment, then said, "I always felt the same way about the desert. It seemed that I could find Him there when I couldn't in the city. Of course, He's there, too, but I know what you mean."

Katie turned to him, searched his eyes in the fading light. "You really do understand, don't you?" The smile was more in his eyes than his mouth as he nodded slowly. "I'm glad you asked to come with me." She shivered, just a little.

He slipped an arm around her shoulders as they began to walk back toward the house. "Me too, but then I knew I would be. For a couple of days now, I've been thinking about—"

He didn't finish what he was going to say, for just then they caught sight of Marge waving to them from a little way down the beach. They could just make out her words over the sound of the wind and water.

"Supper's ready!"

They started to run simultaneously—feeling like carefree children, they confessed to Marge when they came breathlessly up to her.

"Well, I certainly hope your appetites are good," she said. "I may have cooked too much."

Will assured her he'd manfully do his part, and all three climbed the grassy slope to the House together. Marge went on to the kitchen, but Katie stood for a moment in the large livingroom, taking pleasure, as always, in the first sight of it.

The polished oak floors were only partially covered by a sandy-white, fluffy area rug which Katie sat on more often than she stood on it. Her mother's ability to mix old and new was shown to full advantage in this big, gracious room. Katie had come to the conclusion that she was better off sticking to country style, but Marge had the enviable knack of choosing things that were traditional, country, and antique as well as contemporary, and making them seem as though they had always belonged together.

For instance, the brown leather sofa—the chair in Katie's apartment had originally belonged with it—was extremely plain and probably conservative traditional. But when it was joined by a truly fine old Lincoln rocker, an ornate black walnut grandfather clock and a brass and glass coffee table—not to mention full bookshelves and a myriad of green and flowering plants—the effect was marvelous.

Katie called out to her mother fervently, "How wonderful everything looks!"

"It certainly does, Mrs. Holland," added Will, who'd been quietly enjoying not only the house but Katie's pleasure in it. "It's great of you to welcome me when you had no idea I was coming."

Marge, standing in the kitchen doorway, smiled. "Of course you're welcome. Anyone Katie invites is."

Will looked abashed, but not much, as he said, "To tell the truth, I invited myself when Katie told me you lived at the beach, Mrs. Holland."

The smile became laughter. "Well, she didn't say no, I take it! And call me Marge. Come on, I've got the table set in the sunroom instead of the dining room since there are only the three of us, and I thought you'd prefer it, Katie."

A very pleased Katie explained to Will as they followed Marge that the sunroom was just possibly her favorite room. The multitude of profusely flowering geraniums and begonias, ferns of jungle proportions, and a myriad of other plants that perhaps not even Marge could name gave a garden atmosphere to the long room. Not only did it afford a view straight out at the ocean, but north and south as well. As Marge indicated where they were to sit, Katie could tell they would be treated to a spectacular sunset, which illuminated the giant thunderheads with lavender, rose and gold.

The meal itself couldn't have been simpler: clam chowder, oyster crackers, fresh spinach salad, and huckleberry muffins with real butter and wildflower honey. When Marge apologized for not making dessert Will gave a small moan of satisfaction over his fifth muffin and commented that he hoped it wasn't possible to die of overeating, that everything was absolutely perfect.

"Oh, not quite!" Marge exclaimed as she jumped up and went into the livingroom. Suddenly the sound of music softly filled the room. "I forgot to tell you, Katie, I had speakers installed in there."

"Mom, it *is* perfect now!"

"Well, pretty close," Marge admitted. "Now you two sit still. I'd rather do the dishes myself."

"Are you sure?" asked Will.

"She's sure," said Katie. "We take turns, because she says I mess up her system." Marge soon had the table cleared, and Katie fell silent, giving herself to the familiar view. Because of the faint glow lingering in the sky from the lovely sunset, the breakers were faintly visible, rolling inexorably toward the shore. But the haunting, unfamiliar music was so beautiful that she gave up the view, closed her eyes and leaned her head against the back of the chair.

A fine mellow guitar was playing the melody against the background of violins and violas and cellos. An oboe, quietly floating above the melody, gave an almost Oriental air. It was so unbearably lovely...

"Katie, are you all right?"

She opened her eyes to see Will kneeling beside her. "Yes, of course." But her eyes were wet with tears, and he touched her cheek gently with one finger.

"Are you sure?"

He looked so worried she shook her head. "Really, there's nothing wrong. It's just the...the music."

"You mean you're crying because of the music?"

Katie turned her head in embarrassment and didn't see the look on his face. "Isn't that the silliest thing you ever heard of?" she murmured.

He was quiet for a moment, then he said gently, "On the contrary, I think it's wonderful. Don't you know how fine a thing it is to feel that deeply, to be touched by music to the point of tears?"

Head bowed, she said, "It's just so beautiful. I've never heard it before." Another movement, a much livelier one, began just then. Katie smiled, and was rewarded by seeing Will's face relax.

"I'll ask your mother what it is," he said, and went to stand in the lighted doorway. As he talked to Marge about the tape, Katie was able to watch him as closely as she liked, because he was turned slightly from her. He wore Levi's as usual, and a navy-check gingham shirt with a button-down collar. Not a very flashy dresser, she concluded; but the well-worn, well-polished, dark brown loafers on his feet somehow finished off what was nonetheless a well-put-together look. Although his taste in clothes was far from Justin's, Katie decided that she liked the way Will Adams looked very much indeed.

Marge was saying, "I think that tape is the one by a

Spanish guitarist. Mmmm, Rodrigo, if I remember right."

"I didn't know you liked guitar music. Where did you get it?" Katie asked.

Her mother grinned, and the resemblance between mother and daughter was obvious for an instant. "It just came and I tried it and liked it."

"Mother! Do you mean to say you joined another one of those record clubs? I thought you said—"

"I know what I said, but it was such a good deal—"

"That you couldn't pass it up!" Katie laughed. "Mom, I hope that weakness isn't inherited."

"What I'd like to know is if she inherited your cooking skill," put in Will.

"Not really, but maybe she'll learn anyway," said Marge drily. "I'll send the leftover chowder with you."

Later, while Will was stowing a box of delectable leftovers in the car, Katie stood on the front step with Marge, who was watching Will thoughtfully. "Does Justin know about him?"

Suddenly defensive, Katie said, "Does he know what, Mom? There's nothing to know. I've just met Will and besides, he's my instructor, not a date." It seemed to Katie as though she'd been through all this with Sharon.

"Don't get all worked up, Katie. I just asked. How is he with the children? Very good, I'd say from listening to him talk about them."

"Yes, he is. I wish you could watch him with the really young ones. It's unbelievable."

"You haven't told me how you like the preschool. I can see you like the instructor, no matter what you say, but what about his subject?"

"Oh, Mom—" She stopped as she heard Marge's low chuckle. "As a matter of fact, I love being with those kids. They need so much...so much attention and love, things *I* can give them."

There was quiet satisfaction in her mother's voice as

she said, "You may have found your place. I've watched you struggle trying to. And I like that young man, very much. He's quite different from Justin, isn't he?"

Katie was glad that Will came back just then, for more reasons than one. She didn't want to respond to her mother's last statement, nor to admit that she had been unconsciously comparing the two men herself all afternoon. She didn't want to think about that at all.

"Said your good-byes?" he asked. "Marge, it's been great. I certainly hope Katie invites me to come again."

"But I didn't, remember—" Katie stopped, but it was too late. True or not, her words sounded rude.

He grinned, nonetheless. "I know you didn't. But next time you will, won't you?"

"I'll see to it," said Marge, giving Katie one last hug.

On the way home Katie relaxed with that cozy, insular feeling she always experienced in a car at night. Will had offered to drive and she'd gladly relinquished the wheel. When they were well on the way he said, "You were right. I like your mother a lot."

"She's a terrific lady. My best friend, I guess. Oh, Sharon and I get along well, but Mom is the only person in the world who can accept me just like I am, warts and all."

"You have warts? This could make a difference in our relationship," he said in mock alarm.

"You know what I mean. It's not that we never disagree. There have been some monumental *discussions* between us. She's not afraid to say so if she thinks I'm headed in the wrong direction." Katie paused, realizing she'd never put her feelings about the relationship she and her mother shared into words.

"She likes me, and I like her...as people, not just mother and daughter. That's part of it, but I guess the main thing is the way she completely accepts me! She gave a little sigh. "I'm not saying it exactly right."

"Oh, I think you are," said Will. "And I believe God

intends for the marriage relationship to be like that too."

Katie turned away slightly and stared out into the darkness. "It's not always like that, though."

"I know. But it can be, with the right person. You do believe that, don't you?"

For a long time she didn't answer. Then she said, weighing each word, "I'm not sure. I see so many unhappy people trapped in bad marriages, or hurt terribly by broken ones, it makes me afraid..."

Her words had become softer and softer, but he heard them, and reached over and took her hand, squeezing it hard. "Don't be afraid. God wants the best for us, and we can have it. We just have to be patient, and let Him show us what He has for us."

"You sound so sure."

"I am. He's never failed me yet, in small things or big. And they don't get much bigger than choosing the person you want to spend the rest of your life with."

It was raining. The storm that had been brewing while they walked on the beach had followed them. The drops were huge and close together, and he switched the wipers to a higher speed. Back and forth they went, hypnotic in their sound and movement. Katie watched them, wanting to match his quiet assurance, knowing she couldn't. And when he spoke again, she wished he hadn't. The feelings his words generated threatened to inundate her, like the heavy rainfall outside.

"I feel He led you to my classroom, Katie."

"Will, don't—"

His hand on hers was warm. When he took it away she felt cold and shivered a little. "Don't fight it, Katie. Let it happen, and be grateful."

She didn't dare ask him what he meant. It sounded very much like what Justin had said, but she felt it was different somehow—exactly how was beyond her reasoning powers at that moment.

Chapter Five

Katie was up early the next day with the intention of spending the whole morning at the preschool. Her schedule was light, and ordinarily she would have been grateful for the opportunity to spend a quiet morning puttering around the apartment, catching up on chores she sometimes let slide in the chaotic course of life on campus. But she found herself thinking of Robby, who was due for surgery the next day; of Eddie with his winsome smile and love of books; of Julie with her strange fits of anger; and of Mark.

She peeked out the window, saw the sky was clear, and made the monumental decision to leave the yellow umbrella at home. The sight of the contrary yellow umbrella brought back her first encounter with Will Adams. She seemed to be thinking of him more often than their brief acquaintance warranted. His words in the car last night came floating to the surface of her consciousness—*let it happen. Let what happen?*

Suddenly restless, she left the apartment—minus the umbrella—feeling a sweet, reckless joy that was augmented by the sparkling morning sunshine. The daffodils' golden faces were courting the sun, with their less spectacular cousins, the gentle, fragrant narcissuses, nodding alongside more often than not. Surreptitiously Katie picked a half dozen of each from the well-tended beds of the library, thinking how the children would enjoy them.

The children. She could barely remember her days before she had begun at the preschool. What had mattered then? Justin, of course, she told herself firmly. But she was unable to forget the niggling memory of Justin's visit to the preschool. Was Will right? Did the children make Justin uneasy, or worse, and if so, why? He certainly hadn't offered to come back.

She shoved the uncomfortable thought aside as she hurried up the stairs and through the dim halls. With a pleasant feeling of nostalgia she remembered from her own childhood the same odors that permeated these old walls: lots of sweaty little bodies, chalk, pencils, ripe sneakers, apples, and tuna and bologna and peanut butter sandwiches by the score.

The preschool teaching research room was always a noisy nest of activity, but today the pitch seemed even higher. Katie soon found out why. Ellen, who was cuddling Mark on her shoulder, spoke up to Katie as she was hanging up her jacket. "Mark doesn't feel well." She rubbed his back absently, then said in a low, confidential whisper, "We may be getting a new kid today."

"Oh, so that's it. I was wondering what was going on." Unconsciously Katie looked for Will, but he wasn't in either the playroom or the large room where the children ate lunch. "How old is the new one?"

"Four months." Ellen glanced over to the door as Will and a young couple—both of whom looked under thirty—entered the room. Will carried a baby in his arms, and as the three came toward them Ellen added quickly, "They're from Georgia, and they're looking at the school because there are some people in this area who want to adopt the baby."

"You can't mean they—" Katie stopped as Will, a rather fixed smile on his face, held out the baby boy to her.

"Mr. and Mrs. Van Pelt, this is Katie Holland, a student

teacher, and Ellen Kendall, who helps us here in the school more than I could tell you in a week."

Katie murmured something polite, and Ellen did the same, then excused herself, saying Mark needed attention immediately. Still a little shaken by the implication of Ellen's words, Katie asked Mrs. Van Pelt, "What's his name?" The baby's downy head was warm on her shoulder.

"Stacy. I call him Stace." The young mother's words were clear, but her hands betrayed her. They kept twisting in slow, tiny movements held close to her body. Her husband, who had not met Katie's eyes when Will introduced them, put his arm around her shoulders.

"It will be all right, Margaret," he said, his voice low and authoritative. "I promise you it will be all right." He turned to Will, who was standing silently nearby. "Mr. Adams, we appreciate your showing us the school, and we're very favorably impressed. Aren't we, Margaret?"

She nodded, a kind of glazed look in her eyes now as she allowed him to lead her away. Before they reached the door Mr. Van Pelt said, in that deep, resonant voice, "We're going to visit with the Byers some more over lunch and discuss the particulars."

Margaret Van Pelt's voice, small and tentative in comparison with his, drifted back. "Why don't we take Stace with us to lunch?" Her husband bent his head to hers, and his words were not audible to the others. Will stood by, then shook hands and watched them leave before he turned back to where Katie stood.

Katie held Stacy Van Pelt clasped tightly in her arms almost as though she were protecting him from something. "Will, exactly what is going on?"

He saw the anxiety on her face and took her arm, steering her toward his office. Once inside he shut the door, after motioning her to sit down. He sat opposite her, his blue eyes dark and brooding on the baby Katie held. Although she didn't repeat her question, it seemed to hover in the air. Finally Will said slowly,

"The facts are pretty simple. Stacy has been diagnosed as having Down's syndrome, and Mr. Van Pelt feels the baby would be better off in an adoptive home. He's their first child—"

Katie interrupted. "You're saying he intends to give the baby away?" Will nodded his head, not speaking. "But his wife—Stacy's *mother*—does she agree?" It didn't seem possible.

Again, Will took his time answering. "Mr. Van Pelt is a very successful lawyer, and I suppose he's accustomed to persuading people to his point of view."

"But Will, this is not a trial. It's their own child! I can't believe she'd just...just give him away!"

Will sighed. "She didn't really say so, but I don't believe she wants to. However, Mr. Van Pelt feels their marriage won't weather the strain a child like Stacy will inevitably put on it." He met her eyes now. "I know what you're thinking, that you'd never give up your baby, even if he were like Stacy."

"Yes, that is what I'm thinking!" Katie had unconsciously pulled the baby even closer, and he didn't object. He seemed to like being held tight and close. She looked down into his round little face, at the slanting, weak-looking blue eyes and tiny mouth, with its pink tongue protruding slightly from his lips. He was a fair-skinned baby, and she could see milky blue veins under his delicate eyelids. His nose needed wiping. Infinitely vulnerable, totally helpless, and precious beyond words.

Will shook his head. "You mustn't judge them, Katie. People do the best they can with whatever emotional reserves they have. Do you really think you could face raising a child like Stacy? His heart is weak, and already he has respiratory problems. He's going to need an enormous amount of care."

Katie's eyes shone with tears. "No, I'm probably not strong enough to cope with all that, and I don't know how I'd face it." She tried to swallow, found it difficult.

"But I would, somehow I...I would. I'd love him, and just do it."

For a very long moment their eyes met and held. Then he said slowly, "Me too. More than once I've asked myself the same questions and my answers were pretty much what you said. I couldn't do it, but I would." Suddenly his lean face lighted with a smile. "How would you like to work with Stacy if they decide to let the Byers adopt him?"

"Is there a chance they won't?" asked Katie with the naked hope plain in her voice.

Grave again, Will shook his head. "I don't think so. Mr. Van Pelt is convinced their marriage is doomed if they don't start fresh—without the baby."

"Well, I'll tell you this, any man who said I had to choose between him and my child better have his bags packed! If you ask me, the marriage doesn't have a chance anyway." She held the baby out a little, then caught him close again. "That woman won't be able to forget Stacy, and she won't be able to forgive her husband for making her give him up, either."

"You may be right. It's a difficult situation."

Katie's eyes blazed suddenly. "And what if they should have another child, and what if he isn't perfect, either?"

"Hey now, calm down. We can't sit in judgment, you know. The man's handling the problem the best way he can—"

"You may not want to judge him, but I do! And yes, if you'll let me I do want to work with Stacy, and...and love him." She walked quickly to the door, leaving Will staring after her with mixed feelings on his face. Exasperation at her anger at the Van Pelts and admiration bordering on something much stronger at her fierce, loving attitude toward the baby in her arms.

"I'll get you the parents' manual, and we'll work together to develop a program for him," he said as she paused in the doorway.

"All right," she said almost meekly. "Will, I'm sorry to be so...intense. Do you think it's catching?"

Startled, he said, "Down's syndrome? No, of course not. It's a genetic problem, Katie."

She smiled. "I meant your intensity. Do you realize that this is the first thing I've felt this way about since I laid eyes on that Barbie doll of Dad's? And that was a hateful, destructive intensity. This is, or can be, something good. I can really help Stacy, can't I?"

"Yes, Katie, you can. Together we can make a difference in that little boy's life, even if—"

"Even if his mom and dad are preparing to give him away because he doesn't suit their ideas of what their son is supposed to be?" she asked quietly.

He took a deep breath. "It's just not up to us to say whether they're right or wrong. Our job is to see that Stacy is prepared as well as possible to face a world that is still rather hostile to little guys like him. And schools like ours make a real difference."

"That's what I want," said Katie, "to make a real difference in someone's life."

"Oh, you've done that already," Will breathed, but she was moving away and didn't hear him. He sat at his desk for a long time, thoughtfully gazing into space.

As the last of the children were leaving that afternoon, Will walked over to where Katie stood at the window, staring out. Mr. Van Pelt had come for Stacy alone, and it had taken every bit of strength Katie possessed to be polite to him and keep from asking the harsh questions in her mind.

Will didn't touch her as he said, "Are you all right?"

"Of course...no, I guess not really," Katie murmured. "I was thinking just now of my mother." The distress in her voice was evident.

Ellen and a couple of the others came up then, and Will, his voice low, said, "Wait for me outside. I'll walk you home."

Numbly Katie nodded, and once outside she

breathed deeply of the spring air that was so full of promise. What promise did Stacy's future hold? Katie was amazed at the depth of feeling the baby had kindled in her, and the pain those feelings caused. Maybe she wasn't suited for teaching these children after all.

When Will joined her it was those anguished doubts she voiced first. They started walking, his arm loosely around her shoulders. "But Katie, only someone like you, capable of this depth of feeling, can reach our kids. Surely you see that."

"I don't know. All I can see is that at the first hint of something really terrible—like Mr. Van Pelt calmly giving away his firstborn son—I fold!"

He squeezed her shoulder. "You haven't folded and you aren't going to. You're much stronger than you think."

She managed a weak smile as she glanced at him. "You're sure about that, are you?"

"Um hum." He looked up and added, "I'm also sure it's going to rain cats and dogs before we get to your place."

She started to ask how he knew when the first fat drops spattered on the sidewalk, then quickly covered it and them. "We'd better run!" When they reached her house and stood laughing breathlessly on the porch she said, "You're soaked to the skin!"

"And you think you're not?" he retorted, lifting a strand of her damp hair.

"I must look awful. You always seem to see me in my worst moments—" She halted, caught by the sudden look in his eyes.

"You look fine to me," he murmured. "Well, I'd better let you go upstairs and get into some dry clothes."

He made a move to leave, but she took his arm. "I can't let you go back out in that," she said. The rain was still falling steadily. "Come on up until it stops." The indecisiveness on his face was plain, and Katie added, "Please?"

"Now how can I refuse that?"

She laughed and pulled him toward the stairs. "Then don't, and hurry before I freeze!"

The apartment was warm and fairly neat, Katie noted gratefully as she rummaged in the kitchen cupboard. She had found a sweatshirt of her own for Will and he pulled it on, shivering, after shedding his damp shirt and sweater. Working faster in the kitchen than she usually did, she soon had mugs of steaming chicken noodle soup on a tray.

"What's this?" asked Will as she brought it in to where he sat.

"Soup. You seemed to enjoy it at the coffee shop, and I thought it would warm us up."

He grinned as he took a cautious sip. "What I really enjoyed was talking to you. It's not every day I find someone who's so interested in my kids. Now tell me what you started to say about your mother, when we were at the school."

"You don't forget much, do you?" It struck Katie again that Will was an extraordinary man.

"Not if it's important to me, or to someone I care about."

Katie, who'd changed into her favorite at-home outfit—a long, wildly colored but wonderfully embroidered Mexican wedding dress—sat at the other end of the couch. She tucked her feet up, the mug of soup held in both hands for warmth. "Oh, I had just realized that Mr. and Mrs. Van Pelt are not the only ones involved, that Stacy more than likely has grandparents, and…"

"And you wondered how they felt about losing a grandchild, how your mother would feel," said Will thoughtfully. "I'll have to confess that hadn't occurred to me. But it is an important factor. There's bound to be a great deal of conflict in the extended family when parents make the decision Van Pelt has."

"My mother loves babies."

"And she'd love Stacy. That's what you're thinking, isn't it?"

Katie nodded. "Mr. Van Pelt must be a totally selfish man," she said angrily. "Like my father."

"Katie, I wish you could resolve that—" He was interrupted when Sharon burst in the door.

"It's *wet* out there! Katie, did you get caught in it?" She saw Will then, and her face took on an almost comical look of pleased surprise.

"Yes, we did get caught in it," he said. "Want some chicken soup?"

"Katie, did your mother send soup?" Sharon asked eagerly.

With a little laugh Katie said, "Sorry to disappoint you. It's just fresh from the can."

"Well, I'll have some anyway." She stopped suddenly and said, "Unless you two want to be *alone*."

"Sharon, for heaven's sake! You're about as subtle as a Mack truck." Katie shook her head at the slyly suggestive look on Sharon's face. "Get yourself some soup, and come sit with us."

"If you're sure I won't be intruding," she said, her eyes on Will.

"Of course you won't," he said easily. "I've been wanting to get acquainted with you."

As though she'd like to believe him, Sharon murmured on her way to the kitchen, "That's really nice. You're a lot different from some people I know."

It was close to five o'clock when Katie walked downstairs to the door with Will, aware that he didn't want to leave even then; even more aware that she didn't want him to go.

They stood on the porch, gazing out at the clearing, softly sweet, late afternoon. "I'll get your shirt back to you," he said.

"No hurry. Yours is in the bathroom, probably still dripping."

"I should have taken it—"

"No, no, it's fine, I don't mind at all." She breathed deeply of the spring air. "Well, thanks for taking time to let me spout off. You make me feel better about things, even when I can't change them."

She was leaning against the carved post of the veranda, and Will stood close, one hand on the post behind her. His eyes were dark and intense as he said softly, "And you make me feel—" Katie felt suspended, as though the world had stopped. He was so near, all she had to do was reach up and touch his cheek, his hair. But her hand wouldn't move, she couldn't even breathe. Suddenly he said in an altogether different tone, "Thanks again for the soup. It was a pleasant afternoon."

"Yes," agreed Katie faintly as he moved away and gave her a wave of good-bye. He was gone before she could catch her breath. "It was a pleasant afternoon..." she whispered to herself as she slowly climbed upstairs.

That evening Justin surprised Katie, bringing an armload of the daffodils and narcissuses that she loved, and bright red tulips as well. Sharon, her brows raised as high as they'd go, shaking her shaggy head, went off to the kitchen with his offering.

"It was sweet of you to bring flowers, Justin," said Katie. "Extravagant, but sweet."

"I enjoy buying things for you, Kathleen." His eyes took in her faded jeans, bare feet, the sweatshirt that Sharon had been experimenting with by chopping out the sleeves and neck. "Pretty things."

Katie wondered briefly if she should excuse herself and change into something more appropriate, then decided not to. He had dropped in unexpectedly and she resisted the idea of always being in a dither about whether or not he was pleased with what she wore. She lifted her chin a fraction. "Sharon and I were just talking about Mom's birthday next month. You will be able to get away, I hope?"

"I'll do my best. You know that, Kathleen. But you

also know how things come up at work."

Sharon breezed in then, the flowers beautifully, artfully arranged. She was a surprising girl in many ways. "Why don't you put it in your computer, man?" She cheerfully ignored the warning look Katie flashed her.

Justin, however, took her seriously. "I will schedule it, but I just can't be certain. You understand, don't you, Katie?"

Katie wasn't sure she did, but she said, "Of course, Justin, but we'd miss you if you couldn't come. Will and I were down to see Mom yesterday, and I'm sure she's looking forward to seeing you soon, too."

The expression in his gray eyes changed subtly. "Will? Isn't he the instructor at your preschool?"

"Yes," said Katie. "He and Mom hit it off very well."

Justin nodded thoughtfully. "I see. That's...nice."

"Yes, it was." Somehow Katie didn't think it was a brilliant idea to mention that Will had walked her home today, had come in, and that they had such a good time. She glanced at Sharon, whose expression showed she was reading Katie's mind and wasn't about to spill the beans.

Instead she said casually, "Say, Justin, get Katie to tell you the latest development down at the preschool. It'll knock your socks off."

Dutifully Justin asked, "A new development, Kathleen?"

"Yes, a new child, actually." Wishing Sharon hadn't chosen that particular diversion, she gave a quick summary of the Van Pelts' visit to the preschool. It was difficult to keep her feelings about it under control. "They haven't definitely said what they're going to do, but I think Mr. Van Pelt had his mind made up before they came. I also think he wants to be rid of the baby—" She stopped but it was too late. The angry bitterness was in her voice again.

Justin crossed his legs, carefully mindful of the crease

in his trousers. "It's probably the best thing for the child, you know."

"When I think of the father's attitude, I guess it may be. But that still doesn't make it right. And the mother—she loves little Stacy, I could see it in her eyes! How can he make her give up her baby?" Katie's own eyes shone with unshed tears. She hoped desperately they wouldn't spill over.

"Now, you can't let this get you down. You have to remain calm and objective."

"*You* can say that! You didn't hold that baby in your arms and realize he'll never know the love of his mother, never be taught and helped to grow by his father. Why, his father feels he's a hindrance, just something that's come between him and his wife!"

"Katie," put in Sharon, "cool it. Justin's right about one thing—you can't allow this to get you down, or you won't be a help to Stacy, either." The expression on her face showed she regretted bringing the subject up.

Justin held up a hand to Sharon as if to say, let me handle this, and moved over to sit close to Katie, his arm around her. "We need to approach this logically, and rationally."

Sharon, a disgruntled frown on her face, stood up. As she stalked off to her room she muttered, "Excuse me. I know when I'm excess baggage!"

Katie was too distraught to notice, and Justin, who wanted Sharon to leave them alone anyway, was relieved. "Now, Kathleen, surely you can see that everyone can't approach a problem the same way."

She pulled away, staring into his face. "That's the way you see little Stacy, as a problem?"

"I didn't say that at all."

"And I suppose you feel that giving away the problem is a logical, rational decision, and you might do the same?" Her voice was very quiet and dangerously calm now, a fact which Justin was perceptive enough to recognize.

"I really don't know what I'd do, and if you're honest, you'd have to say you don't, either."

"You're wrong, Justin, I know exactly what I'd do." She looked steadily into his eyes. He didn't flinch. Justin was nothing if not courageous and honest.

"It might be best if we let the subject rest for a bit, Kathleen," he said finally. "After all, it's a new situation and you don't know for sure how it will work out." He smiled, and his fingers were insistent as he caressed her arm. "That's an outlandish outfit you're wearing."

"It's Sharon's."

"Oh," he said, "I should have known you didn't buy it."

"You don't like Sharon, do you?" she asked slowly, remembering Will's easy acceptance of her friend.

"Of course, I do," he responded immediately, inclining his head to brush her temple with her lips.

"It doesn't seem like it sometimes." He could be so gentle, so quiet and comforting; she could almost forget their disturbing conversation.

"I just like being with you better—being with you alone." He pulled her close.

When he kissed her, Katie told herself that men like Justin Moore didn't come along every day. He was good, and dependable, and he loved her very much. Why couldn't she make up her mind?

He murmured against her hair, "I'm sorry I can't be certain that the weekend of your mother's birthday will be open. But there are some very important things developing in the office. If I can't make it, will you miss me?"

"Of course, Justin."

He leaned back, a thoughtful look in his gray eyes. "How did you happen to invite your instructor to go to Lincoln City with you?" he asked. The question seemed casual enough.

Katie wasn't fooled, and was glad to be able to say, "I didn't, he invited himself. My car wouldn't start and he came out of the education building and fixed it, and one thing led to another. When I told him I was late—"

"One thing led to another, hmm?"

It was a moment before Katie knew he was teasing, or was he? Justin Moore didn't tease much. "Justin, I hope you don't think I'm the kind of woman who...who fools around!" she said indignantly, wishing she had chosen a more elegant way to phrase that statement. She also felt a twinge of guilt as she remembered those last moments with Will on the porch earlier. After all, nothing had actually happened—*but you wouldn't have minded if it had*—an insistent voice taunted her.

Laughing, he caught her close again. "No, I most certainly do not. I think you're the kind of woman mothers hope their sons will bring home—that's what kind of woman I think you are."

"That sounds dull," she retorted, her voice muffled against his shoulder.

He put his hands on both her shoulders and held her at arm's length, his eyes gazing intently into hers. "Kathleen Leah Holland, you are anything but dull, and I can't imagine what I ever did before I met you." He stood, pulling her to her feet with him. "I'm going to be very busy for the next few weeks, and I might not be able to get over as often as I'd like. But I'll be thinking of you often. Think of me, too, darling."

Katie murmured that of course she would; then chided herself for thinking in the same instant of the look in Will's eyes just before he had left so abruptly that afternoon. She felt that twist of guilt again, and it made her respond to Justin's kiss more warmly than she should have. His arms tightened, his own response ardent. She didn't have the courage to push him away.

Chapter Six

The following weeks flew by so quickly that Katie was amazed. Each day was filled with anticipation, with such a feeling of what's going to happen today that she realized suddenly the term was already more than half over. Up until this term she had just had to grit her teeth and tell herself nothing went on forever, not even semesters, but her attitude was different now. She had started a journal, and one afternoon when she sat down to write she began to read instead.

Eddie was there in the closely written pages. Laughing, boisterous Eddie who worked so hard for each small advance, who enjoyed everything to the fullest, especially the story times he and Katie shared daily. And Robby, who had come back after a two-week absence with his lip still tender from surgery, but who was working mightily to please his speech therapist. He still lapsed into sign language when he was unable to make his mouth say the words. And Julie, who as yet showed no signs of growing out of the unexplained rages that disturbed them all so much.

But it was the Down's syndrome babies who drew Katie the most, especially Stacy. He was very special to her, and she tried hard to convey the love in her heart as she held and cuddled him each day, as she doggedly pursued his program even when it seemed that she wasn't getting anywhere at all. It was as though she wanted to make up to him for losing his parents.

Even now as she read an entry she had written about the day his parents went back to Georgia—without him—she could hear a conversation between several of the workers in the school. It had been at the close of the preschool day, and Will and the others were finishing the daily chore of cleaning up after lunch. Katie sat listening in the rocker with Stacy in her arms and voiced the thought that had come often in the past weeks. "I really wish I knew."

Ellen, whose cheerfulness and total devotion to the children had won Katie's respect and admiration, said, "Knew what, Katie?"

Katie hesitated as she looked down into Stacy's peaceful, sleeping face. Her arms tightened involuntarily. "I just keep wondering if he knows his mother isn't here."

A thoughtful frown wrinkled Ellen's brow. "Gee, I don't know. How old is he?"

"Almost six months." Katie pulled his socks up, wondering if he had any shoes, or if his new mother thought he was more comfortable without.

"What do you think, Will?" asked Ellen as he finished stacking the chairs on top of the table so he could sweep up the lunch litter.

"About what?" He stood easily, hands on his hips, dressed as usual in jeans and a blue plaid shirt with the sleeves rolled up.

"Oh, Katie was wanting to know if Stacy misses his mom and dad, or if he's even aware that they aren't—" She stopped, a funny look on her face. "It's still hard to believe they did it. And it's hard for me to feel right toward them."

Will shrugged. "It's done. And I've found out that the couple who are in the process of adopting him lost a Down's syndrome child of their own."

"Really?" This was news to Ellen. "That makes me feel a little better, but I still wonder."

"If he knows?" Will came over to the rocker and knelt beside it, and with one finger rubbed the soft fuzz on the baby's head. "I'm just not sure. But I..."

When he didn't finish, Katie asked, her voice low and compelling, "What, Will?"

His fingers trailed off the baby's head and touched Katie's arm lightly. "Just that I hope with all my heart that he doesn't."

His words were so soft she doubted if anyone else, even Ellen, had heard, and his brief touch was so slight she was amazed at the sudden surge of feeling through her.

He stood suddenly, including the others in his next statement. "The important thing we have to remember is that Stacy has two parents now who understand his condition and accept it, and that he might otherwise be in an institution."

"But it could have been even better!" burst out Katie.

"I know what you're thinking." Will's gaze was compassionate, and all the others in the room were still as he said, "But it isn't necessarily true that he would be better off with his natural parents, not if they felt as strongly about it as they obviously did."

"It's monstrous, to give away your own—" Katie choked on her words, suddenly aware that she'd wakened Stacy in her vehemence. "There, there, little boy, it's all right." He peered at her, smiling in recognition. He was still smiling when Mrs. Byer came to pick him up. Katie relinquished him reluctantly, searching the quiet, rather plain woman's face for some sign that she loved Stacy. But the woman was evidently not the kind who showed her feelings to strangers. She thanked Katie for caring for Stacy, spoke briefly to Will, and left.

Katie sat in the rocker, not moving even when Ellen and all the others except Will left, too. He went on straightening the room, making notes, tidying up, until finally he came over to her and drew up another chair.

There they sat, almost knee to knee, and he met her

angry, confused stare squarely. "You're still deeply disturbed by this, aren't you?"

His words triggered a violent response. "Yes, I am! I don't see why Stacy should have to go through life with all the problems he has and without his family too. It's wrong!"

Will sighed and reached for her clenched fists. He held them in his big warm hands until her fingers relaxed—and still he held them. "Katie, can you honestly tell me that you believe these strong feelings you've been having aren't conveyed to Stacy?"

"I..." Katie tried, but she couldn't deny it. "No, I can't."

"And don't you agree that it isn't the best thing for him to be cared for every day by someone who's full of anger and resentment?" he persisted gently.

"Yes." The word was small and forlorn. "But I *do* feel strongly about the situation, and I can't help that, can I?"

He challenged her silently, boldly, then said aloud, "Can't you?"

"No, I can't!"

"Not even for Stacy, if not for yourself?"

"I don't know what you mean," Katie said faintly, even as she fought the knowledge.

"I think you do. God knows what's best for us, and He knew when He said we must forgive others. It's not optional, Katie. If you can't forgive the Van Pelts, then God can't forgive you."

"Are you saying God punishes us by refusing forgiveness until we forgive others?"

"No, I'm not."

"Well, it sounds like it."

Her hands were clenching again, and slowly, carefully, he smoothed each finger out until they lay open and loose again in his own. "What I'm trying to say is that when you refuse to forgive someone, you close the door on God—*you* stop the forgiveness He's willing and wanting to give to you."

Katie tried hard to stop the stinging tears, but one escaped. He wiped it away with a knuckled forefinger.

"Then it's all my fault?"

He laughed, startling her so that she drew away. But he caught her hands again and said tenderly, "You sound so pitiful and sorry for yourself."

"That wasn't very nice," she murmured, feeling his knees pressed against her own and unable to break away from his eyes.

"No, it wasn't, and I apologize. I didn't mean to imply any of this was your fault. Of course, it isn't. I only meant that when other people make what we consider bad decisions, even painful or sinful ones, we still have to accept them, forgive them, and love them."

"The Van Pelts too." Small words, falling into the long silence after he'd finished.

"Maybe especially the Van Pelts. Can't you imagine how much they need love right now?"

She smiled for the first time since Mrs. Byer had come for Stacy. "You almost make me wish they lived nearby so I could practice loving them."

"Only almost?" His tone was gently teasing now.

It was her turn to laugh. "Well, what do you expect, a miracle?"

"As a matter of fact, yes," he answered, giving her hands one last squeeze before he let them go. "We see miracles with these kids every day, don't we?"

"Yes, we do." A sigh escaped her, but it wasn't misery now—it was relief. She really did feel better. "Will, you're good for me. I never knew anyone who could make me see things as clearly as you do."

"I'm glad." He was silent for a moment, as though he was thinking. When he spoke again Katie was touched by his words. "Do you think you'd feel better about Stacy if I arranged a visit with his adoptive mother?"

"I'm not sure, Will. You've been there, I take it?"

He nodded. "You'd be surprised."

"Probably. She seems..." Katie hesitated, not wanting to say anything unkind about the woman.

"Distant? Maybe even cool?"

Katie made a regretful face as she nodded. "There I go again, judging her, and I shouldn't."

"I'll make the appointment."

And he had. Katie's journal also held her record of the day when she and Will walked up to a scaled-down version of the house where Katie lived. The wraparound porch was furnished with a hanging swing and a well-used set of wicker furniture. The oval, beveled glass in the front door was shiny clear and revealed an array of green plants in the small foyer as they stood waiting for Mrs. Byer to answer the doorbell.

Her quiet, narrow face registered pleasure at the sight of Will, who said, "Mrs. Byer, you remember Katie Holland from school, don't you?"

"Of course. Come in, both of you. Stacy is asleep, but I've made coffee. We can have some while he finishes his nap." They followed her into a large, pleasant country kitchen which had unmistakable signs of a baby in residence: toys here and there, a beautiful old oak highchair, and a playpen in the sunny corner near the breakfast nook where she seated them.

The coffee she poured was hot and obviously some special blend. Katie sipped it appreciatively and Will talked to the woman as she pulled a pan of delectable looking croissants from the oven.

"I'm impressed, Mrs. Byer. My mother cooks a lot, and she tells me croissants aren't the simplest things to make," said Katie.

Mrs. Byer gave a short laugh. "She's right. And since Stacy came to us there's very little time for baking. It's sort of a hobby of mine, and my husband persuaded me to make these while he played with the baby." Her somber face lit with what could only be love when she spoke of the baby.

"I've seen him with Stacy," said Will between bites of

his flaky croissant. "He's very good with him."

"My husband is one of those men who are meant to be fathers. When our ba—our first baby was born, Sam was the happiest man in the world, until they told us Jon would most likely not live until adolescence because of his heart. We lost him before he was even four years old."

There was such a look of calm acceptance on her face that Katie ventured to ask, "How long was it before you decided you wanted to adopt a child?"

"Oh, I knew right away," said Mrs. Byer. "And I knew I wanted a child like Jon, one who faced the same difficulties and problems."

"But why?" Katie's question was just above a whisper. She desperately hoped the woman would know it wasn't just idle curiosity. In the long moment that passed before Mrs. Byer answered, Katie was acutely aware of the homey comfort of the room, the clean sparkle of the windows, the inviting view into the dining room. Mrs. Byer was a woman who cared lovingly for her home, and Katie wanted to believe the loving care extended to Stacy.

"Because of Jon. Because I know that not everyone is willing, or able to love these children. And they are very, very special." Her eyes, that Katie had thought distant and expressionless, were glowing now. "I loved Jon every bit as much any mother does a normal child, maybe more because he needed more!"

"I see." Katie took a deep breath.

"And I...I still had so very much love to give a child, but Jon died. If you're wondering why we didn't have another baby, it was nine years before I conceived Jon, and the doctors think it's unlikely that I ever could again." A smile turned the corners of her thin mouth up slightly. "My husband and I discussed it, and contacted a group we'd heard about when we were looking for help for Jon—a group that finds prospective parents for children like Stacy."

Katie felt a question buzzing in her brain, pushed it back for a second, then blurted it out. "Mrs. Byer, doesn't it make you angry to think of the Van Pelts giving Stacy away, their own baby?"

"Stacy is *our* baby," Mrs. Byer said firmly. "As far as the Van Pelts go, I'll have to confess I don't think of them at all. Wouldn't you like some more coffee? It's my husband's favorite, a Colombian blend."

"Yes, please," said Katie, stealing a glance at Will, hoping he wasn't seething at her impertinence. Far from seething, he sat completely relaxed in the corner of the nook with a pleased, knowing look on his face. *Why,* thought Katie, a rush of gratitude flowing through her, *he knew exactly what would happen when he brought me here.*

"I'll have another cup too," he said, "or is that Stacy I hear?"

Mrs. Byer glanced upward, and began to walk quickly from the room. "Would you like to see Stacy's room, Miss Holland?"

Katie glanced at Will, who waved her away, saying, "I'll just pour myself another cup of Mr. Byer's Colombian coffee and enjoy it here in this warm sun. You two go on."

Upstairs Katie looked around the pleasant nursery while Mrs. Byer tended the quietly gurgling baby. There was abundant evidence of his every need being anticipated and met, from the fine maple crib to snowy diapers in a neat pile and a low shelf of toys. The fact that most of the things had in all likelihood once belonged to a small boy named Jon didn't seem bad. Far from that, it seemed altogether proper.

When Mrs. Byer had freshly diapered Stacy and put his socks back on, she handed him to Katie, who was convinced he recognized her as he nestled into her shoulder. "He's such a cuddly baby."

"And I love him with all my heart. We both do," Mrs. Byer said in answer to all the unspoken questions in Katie's eyes. "How and why the Van Pelts came to the decision to give him up is not important now."

"I can see that," said Katie against the baby's soft cheek.

"The important thing is that he came to us, and that we want him very much." Mrs. Byer seemed to sense Katie's need to know that Stacy was in the right place.

Katie and Will visited for a while longer, with Will doing most of the talking. It centered around Stacy's progress, and what Mrs. Byer could do to further it. As they left she took Stacy, and although she seemed to have slipped back into her former reticence she pressed Katie's hand warmly.

When they were outside Katie thanked Will for bringing her. His only comment was, "I like to make home calls as often as I can."

Katie laughed softly. "That's not the main reason you came and we both know it. I feel as though the weight of the world has been lifted from me."

"Good. Now if we could only make sure each child like Stacy found people like the Byers."

Katie had decided that very day she would regret not keeping a record of the happenings at the school, and had bought the calico-covered book now in her hands to serve as a journal. She had recorded other things besides the children's progress there. A few words on the page before her conjured up another memory and stopped her reading again. One day Will had said, quite casually, "I've got tickets for the Oregon Symphony this evening. Would you like to go?"

Her eyes lit up. "What are they playing?"

He laughed and shook his head. "Katie, you're irrepressible. Am I to understand that if you like whatever music they happen to be playing you'll go with me, and if you don't, it's no thanks?"

Exasperated, she said, "I didn't mean that at all. I just

wanted to know! Why do you always try to interpret what I say?"

"Because it's fun," he said mischievously.

"Well, don't. If you don't know for sure, ask me and I'll tell you exactly." Then, her curiosity got the best of her. "What *are* they playing?" She hastened to add, "I'd love to go, regardless, but—"

He held up his hands. "John Williams is playing with them, the Rodrigo music." He could tell by her glowing expression that she was pleased. "I'll pick you up at a quarter after six, all right?"

He was very prompt, and somehow she wasn't surprised to see how he was dressed when she opened the door that evening. He didn't have on a tie, but the spotless white turtleneck he wore with the dark blue wool blazer and gray slacks looked surprisingly formal. She was glad she'd worn her favorite rose paisley dress. It swirled about her calves and she felt entirely at ease even in her high heels. Far from minding, Will seemed to like her being tall. And because of that she carried herself differently, more proudly.

As she settled herself beside him after the intermission, he said, "I was watching you as you walked back."

"You were?" she murmured, a trifle disconcerted. She had certainly not been aware that he or anyone else was watching her—only of the enthralling music and what a good time she was having.

"Um hum. And I came to a conclusion." The lights had just dimmed, the musicians had ceased their tuning and there was that sudden, expectant hush before the conductor lifted his baton. He leaned very close and whispered into her ear, "I decided that you're quite a woman."

"Oh, I'm too tall—" she breathed.

"No, you're not. You're—" The baton rose and fell and the third movement began, obscuring most of his last words, "the most beautiful—"

The strains of the music were still tangled with her memories of that evening as she read the terse, unrevealing words in her journal. "Went to hear John Williams play the *'Concierto de Aranjuez'* with W.A. Wonderful performance." And although it wasn't written down, she remembered just as well as the music the question Will had asked her at the door of her apartment before he left.

"Will your friend Justin mind that you went out with me? Or will you tell him?" It was lightly put, but Katie could sense the underlying serious tone in his voice.

"Yes, I'll tell him." She hesitated, then added honestly, "He probably won't like it very much."

"But he's also probably too much of a gentleman to go into a jealous fit."

There was only the dim light provided by an ultra-conservative landlord on the landing where they stood, but Katie was close enough to see Will's eyes. They were very intent for all the lightness in his words. "No, I can't see Justin in a jealous fit, or any other kind of fit for that matter—"

He interrupted suddenly. "If you were my girl, I would."

Katie thought—maybe she hoped—that he was going to kiss her. But he didn't. He just said a brief good night and turned away abruptly, leaving her feeling puzzled.

Even now, after working with him all these weeks, she wasn't sure how he felt. He didn't act any differently at school in the days that followed. He was still friendly, still the most intense, yes, the most exciting man she had ever met.

But when she casually mentioned the concert to Justin, she played the whole evening down to the point of calling it a favor to Will, which wasn't true at all. Perversely, Katie kept hoping Will would ask her out again, and was disappointed when he didn't. The only good thing about it was that she was able to tell Justin "no" when he asked casually, but regularly, if she'd gone out with Will again.

There was another entry in the little journal that Katie had never mentioned to Justin. May 2: *W. A. dropped in tonight. He brought me a tape of John Williams playing the Rodrigo concerto...we played Scrabble. He and Sharon really hit it off.*

It had been Sharon's idea to play Scrabble. Katie suspected Sharon was testing Will, who passed with flying colors. He hadn't beaten them too badly and was more than willing to talk about his nephew Tommy and the kids at school with Sharon. Her gray eyes had been wide with interest, her legs in a more-or-less lotus position as she sat opposite Will on the floor, the Scrabble board between them. "So you decided Tommy *could* tie his shoes—"

"Yes, after I read a book that says there are fifty-seven different steps for teaching a child with learning disabilities to tie his own shoes."

"Fifty-seven?"

"Right. That's one of the keys, and it's called the task-analysis approach. You break skills down to their simplest terms, start at the beginning, and have the children do them over and over and over. They *can* learn."

"Anyone? Even those who seem beyond help?"

He nodded.

"That's incredible!"

"You're right. But it proves what I've heard countless times, paraphrased by educators in all kinds of ways. Anyone *can* learn. Wasn't it Socrates who said that first?" He grinned, taking away any sound of pomposity.

Katie had heard all this but to see Will explaining it so carefully to Sharon added another dimension to her respect for him. She found herself comparing him with Justin more and more, and becoming more and more confused about her feelings.

She sighed and closed the journal, glad she was going to her mother's on Friday. She badly needed some time to walk on the beach and let the ocean work its magic.

Chapter Seven

Friday dawned clear and especially bright, and grew even better as the day gently unfolded—spring at its best. Will succumbed to the suggestion that the staff go outside for their end-of-the-week faculty meeting, knowing full well that spring fever was rampant among them. The lure of the warm sun, the soft, scented air, that indefinable something that makes people foolish and happy for no reason—for every reason—was too much to resist. Springtime in the Willamette Valley is almost always extravagant. Today a riot of golden forsythia and lavish lilac in shades from creamy white to deep lavender pervaded the air with a heady fragrance which made Katie dreamy.

The whole crew lounged on the grass as Will spoke, earnest and intense as always. Katie, who held Robby in her lap because his mother was late, sat a little apart from the others, thinking Robby's mother could collect him easier that way. From time to time she murmured to him, "I love you, Robby. Can you say, I love you, teacher?"

He grinned and ducked his head, then made the sign for cat. Katie whispered, "No, you don't. Say cat. C-c-cat." Even though Garbage Cat had gone wherever stray cats go in the spring, Robby hadn't forgotten him. He tried valiantly to form the sound, then made the sign again, begging with his eyes for acceptance. She gave in this time, saying, "You'll get it, sweetie. We won't quit until you do. I promise."

His mother came around the corner of the building, an apologetic smile on her face. "I'm sorry I'm late—"

"It's okay, really," whispered Katie. "I thought about taking him home with me, but I decided you would come for us both." She dropped a kiss on Robby's woolly head.

The harried-looking young mother stared into Katie's eyes for a moment, then said, "I don't know what I'd do if all of you didn't care about Robby too, if I didn't have help...if the school wasn't here."

Touched by the depth of emotion in her voice, Katie patted her arm. "We love him, too."

The woman nodded gratefully as she took Robby, who waved gaily at the group. Will called out, "See you Monday, sport!" and went on with his explanation.

Katie, free now to pay attention to Will, did just that. But her mind was not really on what he was saying. She kept thinking how blue his eyes were, how expressively he used his hands. It was as though his hands had a language of their own as he used them to illustrate his spoken words.

So deep was she in her own thoughts that Katie was startled when Will rose and looked straight at her. "Don't you agree, Katie?"

"What?" Katie was forced to admit, "I'm afraid I wasn't paying attention."

He laughed and so did all the others. "I can take a hint. We'd better dismiss before I lose the rest of you to spring fever."

They all stood lazily and drifted away, teasing Katie a little, but also admitting they felt it too—that itchy, dreamy, unsettling ferment.

When only Will was left, still sorting and stacking his inevitable papers, she went over to him. "Will, I want to apologize."

His eyes were laughing. "It's all right, really it is. But I could have sworn you were looking straight at me."

She had been, that was true, just as she was now, and the nearness of him made it impossible to look away. "I—" She stopped, because she had no idea what she wanted to say.

He seemed to be having the same problem, and for a few moments they just stood, looking into each other's eyes, until he said, "The weather is so terrific that it must be good even in Lincoln City."

"Could be, but you know what they say, 'If it's nice here, it's stormy there and if it's raining here, it's—' "

He broke in. "Sunny there? Is that what they say?" She nodded, and finally he said slowly, "Does it matter, though?"

"Not to me, any weather is good weather. I love it when it storms on the beach."

"I like a positive woman." His face showed signs of some sort of indecision, but he threw up his hands, as if in defeat. "Well, it worked once—I'll try again. I've got the whole weekend ahead with absolutely nothing to do. What would you say if I volunteered to drive you over to see your mom, Holland House, and *your* ocean?"

"That's a great idea! Today is Mom's birthday and—" Katie stopped suddenly, but he didn't notice.

"Oh, then I'd better have some advice about a present. And I'll have you know I'm no slouch at baking birthday cakes, either." He was stacking his folders and papers and didn't see the look of consternation on her face for a moment. When he did glance up he said, "Katie, what's wrong?"

"Oh, Will, Justin is supposed to go with me...I forgot." How could she have forgotten?

Evidently Will wondered how she could have, too, because although he was polite, his face was perplexed. "It's okay."

The very politeness of his words made her feel even worse. "I'm sorry..."

"Nothing to be sorry about. I should learn not to go around inviting myself."

"But I like it when you do." Katie felt miserable; partly because she'd allowed the awkward situation to happen, partly because the idea of his going had seemed a very pleasant prospect.

He started inside, his polite smile firmly in place. "Tell your mother I send her my best, Katie. I'll see you on Monday."

There was nothing Katie could do but give him a stiff polite smile of her own and say, "See you on Monday."

She was still feeling as though she'd badly botched the matter when she got home. For the first time she could remember she moped at her packing and couldn't find any pleasure in wrapping her mother's gift—a rosewood pen and a box of note cards made by the kids at the preschool. The cards were really very pretty and cleverly done. Each child dropped pieces of different colored crayons on a heated pie plate that melted them to blended, bright liquid. Then the children pressed pieces of stiff white paper onto the plate. They made a nice little gift.

Even with her reluctant pace she was ready to go shortly before one-thirty, the time she and Justin had arranged to leave. Justin was always prompt, and when he failed to arrive by two o'clock Katie began to worry. At two-thirty she called his office, only to be told he was in a conference, not to be disturbed under *any* circumstances. Katie waited another half hour and called back.

"Yes, Kathleen, what is it?" His voice was not gruff, but there was a hint of, *whatever it is, it had better be important*.

Perplexed, Katie said, "Justin, did you forget that you were supposed to pick me up at one-thirty this afternoon?"

"Why, no, of course not. I left my secretary a note

that she was to call and let you know I'm going to be tied up for the rest of the afternoon."

"She didn't call, and I was beginning to worry."

"What? Please excuse me for a moment, Kathleen."

She could hear muffled snatches of the conversation between Justin and the hapless girl. Katie felt sorry for her and a little angry at Justin for not taking the time to make the call himself.

"Kathleen?" His tone had changed from severe to warm and apologetic. "There's been a mix-up, I'm afraid. Angela was to have phoned you this morning. I'm really sorry."

"Then you can't come at all?"

"No, I'm afraid not."

"But, Justin, it's Mom's birthday!"

"It can't be helped, Kathleen," he said in the soothing tone he might use with a disappointed child. "Something very important has come up. You do understand, don't you?"

"Of course, Justin. Mom will be sorry you can't make it." *Now, Katie,* she chided herself, *that sounds as though you aren't sorry at all—childish, childish, childish!*

"Tell her I send my love." He added, his voice lowered, "To you, too. I have to go, dear."

When he hung up Katie stood for a long time, peeved beyond words. *He should have called me himself,* she fumed, *pushing it off on his poor secretary then bawling her out for not doing something he should have.* Suddenly a little smile curved her lips, and she began to gather up her things. After two trips she had them stowed in her car. With a deep breath and a look of equal parts of apprehension and defiance, she drove across town to Will Adams' apartment and rang the bell before she could change her mind.

"Why, Katie," he said as he opened the door and saw her standing there, "what are you doing here?"

"I came to get you. How long would it take for you to

get ready to spend the weekend at Mom's?"

He stood aside and waved her in. "Oh, about ten minutes, four of which you'll probably use to explain what's going on."

"Justin is busy. His secretary forgot to call, and I waited for over an hour, and he was too busy to talk when I called to see what had happened—" She was aware of sounding childish again, and chagrined to discover she was near tears.

"So you thought you'd show him and invite someone else?" he asked quietly.

"I...I suppose so." Her shoulders slumped. It did sound rather bad when he said it like that. "But you wanted to go, didn't you?"

He nodded slowly. "Yes, I did."

"Don't you still?"

He didn't quite smile, but almost. "Yes."

"Then come with me. Forget that I forgot I asked Justin first, and his secretary forgot to tell me, and let's go!"

He did smile, then. "Katie, you're something else."

"Please?"

"Give me a few minutes."

"Six, you said you only needed six." She looked around her for the first time. "Interesting, very interesting."

He shrugged. "I suppose you could call it charmingly eclectic, but the truth is, it's a fine cross between early New Mexican boyhood and negligent bachelorhood."

"I like it." On the cream-colored walls, the bare floors, even on the furniture were fine examples of Navajo rugs, their bold designs executed in brown and crimson, sand and turquoise, making vivid accents in an otherwise rather austere room. The furniture was mostly old oak mission pieces, except for a nubbly beige sofa and a deep chocolate-brown armchair, which was draped with a rug—as well as a shirt, a pair of jeans, sweat pants, and three socks.

Will hastened to gather up his things, but she said, "Don't bother, go pack."

"If I'd known you were coming, I would have picked up. I'm not a slob, really I'm not."

His earnestness as he stood with his assorted belongings hanging over his arms was almost comic. As always the intensity fairly shone out from him.

"Will, don't worry about it. You don't have to impress me."

"Oh, don't I?" he drawled.

She took a step toward him, saw the arrested look in his eyes and stopped. "No, you don't, because you did that a long time ago." He looked so vulnerable, with socks and sweat pants dangling, that she added softly, "In the classroom with your kids."

"Our kids." His voice was as soft as her own. "Isn't that right, Katie? They're yours too, now."

"Yes. I can't imagine what I lived for before I found them…" *And you,* echoed in her mind. Instead she said brightly, "If you don't hurry up and get ready, I won't have time for my long walk on the beach. You wouldn't want to be responsible for depriving me of that, now would you?"

"No, I sure wouldn't. I'll only be a minute. Four minutes." He still didn't move. It was as though there were invisible cords binding them, drawing them closer. Then he shook his head as if to clear it. "Sit down; make yourself comfortable." He disappeared into the bedroom, leaving her alone.

Katie didn't sit down. She prowled restlessly around the room, pausing to admire an ironwood sculpture of an eagle in flight. She picked it up, marveling at its smooth surface, at the contradictory weight of the bird, its wide wingspread. There was also a collection of rough, unpolished turquoise, and a framed display of arrowheads.

But what drew and riveted her attention was an oil painting of a small band of Indians on the move beneath a vast expanse of sky. There were women and children as well as braves mounted on horses, but the expression on their faces haunted her even when she turned away from it. Katie always reacted to paintings in one way or another—either with a cold shrug, or with her whole warm self.

"Do you like it?"

Will's voice startled her; she hadn't known he was in the room. "I'm not sure. It disturbs me, because I get the feeling there is someone hounding them, chasing them, even though no enemy is in the picture."

He nodded soberly. "In a way you're right. They're on the way to the reservation. Their life as they and generations before them had always known it was coming to an end."

"It shows in their faces. How do you bear it?" Katie felt almost overcome with sadness.

He smiled suddenly and slung his duffle bag over one shoulder. "Let's go and I'll tell you."

Outside in the sunshine she felt a little better. It wasn't until he had transferred her bags to his ancient pickup and they were on their way that he explained to her about the painting and her sadness lifted.

"You see," he was saying earnestly as they pulled onto the highway, "the fate of those once-proud people makes me remember every time I look at the picture that I must not impose my will on others." He grinned and gave her a sidelong glance. "No pun intended, as they say."

Katie returned his grin. "As they say, none taken."

"Anyway, to me it represents the ultimate outcome of one person, or a group or country, for that matter, deciding they have the ability or right to control others."

"I see," she said quietly. "But why not a happier picture? Maybe one of the Indians in better times?"

"We don't learn from the happy times, Katie. We learn from the hard, bad ones. Haven't you found that to be true?"

"I suppose." Somehow Katie didn't want to go on with this conversation, she didn't want to explore the possibilities. So she said, determinedly cheerful, "Are you looking forward to the weekend? I am."

"Yes, I am, even under the circumstances. I'm not sure it's wise, but we won't worry about that now, will we?"

Katie had a sudden, unwelcome thought: *what if by some chance—it would have to be chance, she certainly had no intentions of telling him—Justin were to find out she'd asked Will to come in his stead?* "Absolutely not," she said aloud, "absolutely not."

As always, the House welcomed them. Marge had outdone herself, spring cleaning, then filling every room with spring flowers. Just walking through the rooms was a celebration.

"Mom, everything looks wonderful!" enthused Katie after she and Will had disposed of their bags, his in a room overlooking the beach, Katie's in her attic.

"It certainly does, Marge," said Will. "And it's great of you to welcome me when you had no idea I was coming—again."

"Justin couldn't make it, so I asked Will," said Katie, as if it had been a simple thing.

"Have you met Justin, Will?" asked Marge.

"Yes, he came by for Katie one day at the preschool." Will, his feet propped comfortably on a low hassock, looked perfectly at home despite the shakiness of his invitation. "What are you cooking? I keep catching whiffs of something that's driving me crazy."

Marge laughed. "I've cooked all my favorites, since it's my birthday."

Katie made a wry face. "That's exactly why I should have done the cooking."

"Nonsense, I enjoyed it. We're having guacamole, chicken enchiladas, refried beans, spanish rice with lots of green chiles the way Katie likes it, and taco salad, because I'm hopeless at regular tacos—"

"Stop, I'm not sure I can wait!" Will laughed too, but he looked as though he meant it. "I haven't had any good Mexican food since I left Santa Fe."

"Then come on out to the kitchen and I'll let you pass judgment on my salsa." Marge stood up, graceful and chic in a slim, bright blue, Hawaiian-print dress. "That is, I'll let you if you'll tear the lettuce for the salad."

"Blackmail, pure and simple," grumbled Will, but he was already halfway to the kitchen, eagerness on his face. "Katie, are you coming?"

She studied his face for a moment, saw how completely at ease he was at the prospect of being with her mother, and shook her head. "Remember, I haven't had my walk yet."

Marge looked at her watch. "And you've been here—oh, almost twenty minutes! That's some sort of record, I'd say, isn't it? Well, since I've got a replacement for you in the kitchen, you go on."

"You're sure it's all right?" But they were already leaving the room together, Will rhapsodizing about the aroma of the enchiladas. Katie asked herself if she wanted Will to come with her, or did she want him to get better acquainted with her mother? As she pulled a sweater from the hall closet she heard Will's deep laughter mingle with her mother's throaty chuckle and knew that selfishly she wanted both. She wanted Will to like her mother and even more, for Marge to like him. And, she wanted him beside her, sharing her joy of the sea.

When she reached the beach, the sun was playing hide-and-seek with a few harmless-looking white clouds. Katie decided it was all right after all if Will didn't walk with her. She had a great deal to think about—things she'd been putting off. Drawn by the promise of a fine, clear weekend, an unusual number of people were wandering up and down her beach. They were sufficiently distracting so that she walked to her favorite spot and back without really coming to grips with the issues. After all, Will certainly hadn't said anything definite about his feelings, and when it came right down to it Justin hadn't actually proposed either.

But as she trudged closer to the House she knew all too well that was because she'd begged so often to be given more time, and Justin, gentleman that he was, had honored her request. She had the uneasy feeling that things could not go on much longer as they were, and the reason, plain and simple, was Will Adams. For as she picked her way up the rocky slope she saw him waving to her, and was dismayed at the leap of gladness she felt.

Will had not been boasting idly when he said he was good at baking birthday cakes. By the time Katie entered the kitchen and found an apron to start one, Will, a smug look-what-I-did grin on his face, carefully opened the oven door and invited her to peek in at the nicely rising bundt cake.

"How in the world did you get that done?" she asked incredulously.

"You do take long walks." He shrugged as though, after all, it was nothing, and leaned over to whisper, "It's a mix, and I probably never will manage layers, mix or not. They always sort of lop from side to side, if you know what I mean."

"Do I!" Katie suppressed a giggle. "I'm a recognized authority on lopsided cakes. Say, how'd you ever persuade Mom to let you perform on her stage? She's particular about who cooks in here."

"I promised I'd clean up after myself. Maybe you'd better inspect." He touched the cake with a light finger, then closed the oven door gently.

Katie looked around at the spotless kitchen. Even more than the rest of the house, it was a mix of old and new. There was the large, black restaurant stove that had seen plenty of use before Marge decided she needed to add an even larger one, a huge chopping block that wore the signs of its hundred-years-plus use gracefully, antique teapots and flow-blue china in open cupboards. Over the center island there was an iron rack from which hung the most modern cookware available, plus every cooking utensil devised by man, or so it seemed to Katie, whose cooking ability lagged not far behind Will's.

"Did Mom tell you she not only caters, she also gives cooking demonstrations?"

A woebegone look broke on his face. "And I used a mix—"

"Don't worry, she's not critical. By the way, where did you get it, anyway? I don't think she keeps any in the cupboard."

"If you mean the cake mix, I brought it with me from *my* cupboard. That's all I ever have," he said wryly.

Katie smiled. "I can tell you for sure that she'll like it. Mom is really big on people being thoughtful."

In the silence that followed, Katie could hear the slow tick, tick, tick of the grandfather clock all the way from the livingroom. He was looking at her steadily, and finally he said, "How about you? What's important to you, Katie?"

"Why, the same things that are to her, I suppose." She frowned. There was something in his tone that made her ask, "What are you getting at, Will?"

He leaned against the counter, arms folded on his chest, blue eyes thoughtful. "I suppose what I'm trying to ask is what kind of qualities do you look for in a man."

For an instant Katie was tempted to joke and say, tall dark and handsome, like you, but she saw that he was serious. "I never really thought about it very much." It came to her that she hadn't dated many men before she met Justin, who had carefully shaped and molded her ideas and opinions for a long time now. And she'd gone along, accepting whatever he said as right and proper for her.

Softly, very deliberately, Will said, "I'd like to know."

"Well, I suppose that he should believe the same

things about God that I do—"

When she stopped he nodded encouragingly. "That's a good start, go on."

But she couldn't, for she knew suddenly that whatever she said would be a parroting of Justin, that she hadn't done very much of her own thinking for a very long while. "I guess I need time to think about it, Will."

"That's a good idea. And after you do, we'll talk about it. All right?"

He was gazing at her intently, his eyes almost hypnotic.

"We'll talk about it," she agreed slowly.

Chapter Eight

The birthday cake was a great success, not only because Marge Holland was a gracious lady, but because, mix or not, it happened to be a very good cake. Will tried insisting that she let him and Katie do the dishes after dinner, also a great success, but Marge shook her head firmly.

"And take a chance on you dropping a piece of my china?" The teasing note in her voice took any hint of insult from the words. "Besides, there's a moon rising, and if there's one thing Katie likes better than a walk on the beach in the daytime, it's a moonlight walk." At the look on Katie's face she added, "Minus tide at eight-thirty, daughter."

"Really?" said Katie, her eyes wide with excitement.

"Excuse me, but could an old desert man ask what minus tide means?" Will asked.

As Katie explained, she was already pulling on her favorite old wool sweater and walking out the door. Will followed her, calling back, "I don't drop dishes often—"

Marge laughed. "I didn't think you did! It's just that I tend to be the Lone Ranger in my kitchen. Go on. It's lovely out."

And it was. Katie and Will walked in companionable silence for a long way on the extraordinarily wide, smooth beach, savoring the sight of the waves lit with mirrored silver. Will, his voice hushed, said, "I begin to understand why it means so much for you to come here."

"I never, never get tired of it," Katie breathed. "That God created such incredible beauty makes me absolutely certain that He loves us—and me, especially. All those words we learned in Bible school when we were kids—majestic, omnipotent, omniscient—and He never changes."

"Those are mighty lofty thoughts for a Katy-did."

She could hear the smile in his words even though she wasn't looking into his face. Suddenly she stopped, wanting very much to see him. "Will, you think I'm flighty, don't you?"

"Did I ever say that?"

"No, but I feel..." She trailed off, then said, "You call me Katie."

For a moment he looked taken aback, then he said, "Your mother does, too, and everyone else I know."

"Justin doesn't."

"I see," he said thoughtfully. "And you think that means he takes you more seriously than I do?"

Instead of answering him Katie started walking again. Not fast, but a sudden restlessness made her want to move away from Will, away from even her own thoughts. She was several hundred feet down the beach when she heard his quick running steps behind her. Some totally unexplainable urge struck her and she began to run, too. She ran until she was gasping for breath and felt frantic inside. It was as though some terrible unknown danger would overtake her if she stopped running—and she knew it was only Will.

He caught her just as she was about to run, unseeing, into a shallow but very wide tidepool. "Katie! What's got into you?"

She struggled, still caught in that inexplicable hysteria. "Let me go!"

"No, I won't let you go, not until you tell me what's wrong!" He pulled her close, held her as tightly as he could, with both arms wrapped around her trembling body. "Katie, don't, please."

"Justin calls me Kathleen, he always...always calls me Kathleen." Her breathing was ragged and painful sounding.

Will didn't say anything for a long, long moment. And when he did speak his voice was low, almost hesitant. "You think I don't take you seriously? Oh, you're wrong there, how wrong you are." She had calmed somewhat, and he looked down at her face, turning her slightly so that the moonlight illuminated it more fully. Still holding her tightly with one arm, he brushed the tears from her cheeks, traced the curve of her jaw with damp fingers.

"Honey, I take you so seriously that sometimes I catch myself watching you hug Stacy or Robby, with that sweet tenderness in your eyes, and I wonder what it would be like if you looked at me that way. I convince myself there isn't any such person as Justin Moore, that if I kissed you, you'd be glad."

Katie was quiet now. The shivering panic was gone. His face was shadowed, but what she could see in it frightened and excited her at the same time. "Will..." His head bent to hers, and just when she closed her eyes she never knew. All she knew was the blaze of feeling that tore through her at the warm touch of his lips on hers. Never had she felt anything like it in her life. It raced through her—like a grass fire she'd watched in horrified fascination once. "Will..."

He laughed, as breathless as she felt. "You said that—" His arms still tight around her, he bent to kiss her again, then stopped abruptly. They both stiffened at the sound of someone quite near.

"Kathleen, is that you?" It was Justin.

Katie pulled away, but Will placed an arm around her

waist. Rather than struggle she was still. "Justin, I'm surprised to see you—"

"I can see that."

"But this...it isn't what it seems," Katie said in dismay.

"Isn't it?" asked Will quietly. He tried to look into her eyes but she twisted away. "Katie, don't do this, please. If ever in your life there was a time for honesty, this is it."

"I think you'd better leave, Mr. Adams," said Justin.

"Only if that's what Katie wants." Will's voice was very quiet, perhaps too quiet.

"Oh, Will," Katie wailed.

"Can't you see you're only making matters worse?" Justin said angrily to Will.

But Will stood his ground. "I'm not the intruder here, Mr. Moore, and I'll leave only if Katie says that's what she wants," he repeated.

His arm slipped from her waist, and Katie moved a little apart from them both. The shaking feeling within her wasn't obvious, but she thought perhaps it was, and clasped her body with crossed arms. "Maybe...it might be best if you did leave, Will."

"Are you sure?" Will made no move to touch her, but he looked steadily at her as he waited for her to answer.

Finally she stammered, "I...I suppose. I'm sorry, Will," she finished lamely.

"Don't be, Katie. I'm not sorry, for anything." He turned on his heel and strode away, not touching her, not looking back.

For a long moment Katie and Justin didn't speak. They watched Will's tall, retreating figure until it grew small, then turned up toward the House and disappeared.

"Are you in love with him?" Justin's quiet question broke the long silence.

Had he not phrased it so abruptly she might have been able to explain how she felt, she might have been able to examine her exact emotions and be more honest. Instead she blurted, "In *love* with him? What do you think I am, Justin? How can you even ask that when we're practically—"

"Engaged?" he supplied when she faltered. He came a step closer. "It's time we settled things between us. All this would never have happened if I hadn't let you put it off. You know that, don't you?"

She nodded almost imperceptibly. How could she disagree? "Yes, I know that."

"I've tried to be patient and give you the time you said you needed. But to find you in another man's arms, to think you might slip away from me is something I'm not sure I can cope with."

Katie heard the agitation in his usually calm voice, and it wrenched her heart to think she was the cause. "Justin, please believe me. This is the first time anything like that has happened between Will and me!"

"Of course I do, if you say so." He moved near enough to reach for her and pulled her close. "And I'll believe you if you tell me it won't happen again."

The appeal in his voice was subtle, but unmistakable as he caressed her shoulder in that gentle way he had. It was always so safe, so secure in Justin's arms. No wild, confusing, uncontrolled fire. She stood quietly, trying to rouse her mind from the strange stupor it seemed to have sunk into. How could this be happening so soon after...Will? But one fact was inescapably true—she knew that Justin trusted her, believed her, loved her.

As though he heard her thoughts he murmured, "I've loved you for so long. And you love me, I know it. Say it, Kathleen, don't put off saying it any longer, please."

For an instant Katie panicked. How could she say those words when she had so recently been in another man's arms? A man who kindled emotions she'd never felt before, who made her feel so alive? But she was torn by another thought. She did love Justin Moore. How could she not love him? He had been a part of her life for such a long time, and he was so many things she admired in a man—strong, successful, steady. In a voice that didn't seem like her own, she heard herself whisper, "Yes, I do love you—"

He caught her close again and said exultantly. "I knew it! And you know what the next thing I want to ask is, don't you?"

Katie did, indeed, know, and she felt the panic rising again. "Oh, Justin, please, not now—"

His face, so near her own, grew still. "Kathleen, you can't expect me to wait forever. I want to marry you, and I've certainly not made any secret of it. You know that."

"Yes," she whispered. "But don't ask me to give you an answer right now."

"Why not? Are you sure it isn't that teacher?" When she was silent he asked, "You've told me you aren't in love with him."

She hadn't exactly said that and she knew it. Carefully she began, "I'm...Justin, I'm confused, about a lot of things. Since I started working in the preschool—"

He interrupted thoughtfully. "Since you've been working in the preschool you're different. It's changed you, and I'm not sure it's for the better."

"Why do you say that?"

"Oh, I suppose I'm a little jealous," he admitted. "You seem to be totally involved with those children, not to mention Adams. And I don't mind telling you it was a considerable shock to come upon the two of you like...like that."

"I'm sorry, really I am," Katie said, her voice low. "About Will, I mean. But the children are something else. They give me—" She broke off, then tried again to put her thoughts into words. "They help me define myself, I think. When I'm working with them I feel as though what I'm doing means something, is truly important." Katie felt a little surge of triumph. In trying to explain to Justin she had finally understood what had been happening to her. Her elation was short-lived, however, as he spoke.

"It's one thing to get an education, to pursue a career, even. But Kathleen, it's quite another to let it rule your mind and heart. It's also obvious to me that you've entangled your emotions and your work, that Will Adams has taken advantage of your empathy for the children. Can't you see that?"

She turned away from him and stared out at the silver-frosted whitecaps. They looked as restless as she felt. What she wanted to say was, *"But, Justin, isn't that the way you are about your career?"* Instead she said aloud, "I need a little more time to sort out my thoughts."

He took his time framing a reply. "Kathleen, I told you once I'm a patient man, and I am. But I'm also a clear-headed man, and I pride myself on being a realist. I'm not sure it's time that you need."

Katie couldn't bring herself to say anything but a slightly desperate, "Please?"

He shrugged, and his hand on her shoulder was light. "All right. I have to be out of town all next week. That's another thing I wanted to tell you, when I decided to come down after all. I was preoccupied when you called today and forgot to mention it."

"You're going to be gone all week?" Guiltily Katie realized she was relieved at this news.

"Yes. An important business meeting in San Francisco that could affect my career, my life." He hesitated, then said, "I hope it will be *our* life together."

"When will you be coming back?"

"Saturday. We'll go somewhere special that evening, all right?" She nodded, and he added casually, "It's probably just as well. I didn't bring the ring with me, anyway."

Katie had no answer to that, and when he began walking back toward the House she fell into step silently.

Marge didn't seem surprised that her daughter had left with one man and returned with another, and offered to take Katie back on Sunday rather than have her cut her visit short.

"I only came for the evening," Justin explained. "We have another very important meeting early in the morning."

"On Saturday?" asked Marge politely.

He nodded. "These things can't wait. Kathleen, will you walk me to my car?"

Katie came over to him with a fixed smile, and allowed him to put his arm around her and lead her out the door. Once outside he kissed her more deeply, more passionately than he ever had. Justin either didn't notice her stillness, her lack of response, or if he did, chose not to say anything. She stood in the driveway for a long while after he left, then went back up to the porch.

"Sit down, Katie." Her mother's shadowy figure was just visible at the far end.

"Okay, Mom." She almost laughed—she had the sudden image of herself as a very realistic robot, subject to the whims and orders of anyone who knew which buttons to push. Her mother had said sit, so she sat. Justin had instructed, say I love you, so she said I love you. And Will had pushed her passion-panic button and she'd panicked passionately. Suddenly she did laugh. She laughed until the tears came, then dry, wracking sobs. Marge came over and knelt beside the old wicker rocker where she sat, not touching Katie, but close enough to.

"Cry it out, Katie, cry it out. You haven't cried in a long time, have you?" Katie shook her head wordlessly, and Marge put her arms around her then. They sat like that until Katie quieted. "If you want to tell me, fine. If not, fine. But I would have thought you'd feel just a bit better having two handsome young swains at your beck and call," Marge said wryly.

"You'd think so, wouldn't you," agreed Katie with a little hiccup. "Mom, can you believe that Will Adams kissed me for the first time tonight and I thought I was going up in flames? And not ten minutes later I didn't say yes, and I didn't say no to a proposal from Justin that I've been—" She stopped, not willing to go on.

"Sidestepping for a year?" suggested her mother gently.

A great gusty sigh from Katie joined the breeze that was drifting in from the sea. Far, far out she could see the light from a large ship passing slowly. She watched it until it was quite a distance north of them. "Mom, you've known Justin almost as long as I have."

"Yes, that's true." Marge had a way of saying so much, no more, and tossing the ball back into Katie's court.

But Katie was too exhausted to be anything but direct. "What's your opinion of him?"

"In what capacity? As a computer what'sit, I imagine he's as bright as they come."

"You know what I mean," said Katie in exasperation.

"Yes, I do, and I don't know why you're asking me. I'm not the one who has to make the decision whether or not to marry him.

"But I care what you think," persisted Katie. "About men, about marriage..."

Marge drew her knees up, clasped them with her arms and stared out at the sea. "You're not going to let me off this time, are you?"

"No," said Katie resolutely. But at the sight of her mother huddled at her feet she relented. "Oh, Mom, what you said goes for me, too. If you don't want to talk about it, that's okay. But I'm so confused I need help from somewhere."

Marge stared out at the ocean for a very long time before she spoke. "Will Adams is a lot like your father, Katie."

Such a simple statement. Katie heard it, took it into her mind, then turned it over and over. "Why didn't I see that?" she whispered, almost as though Marge wasn't there.

"You didn't want to. We were both hurt badly. I can imagine that you wanted to forget him as much as possible. And remember, I saw your father several times during the divorce proceedings, but unless I'm mistaken you haven't since—"

"Since that day he brought *her* here."

Shocked at the terrible bitterness in Katie's voice she said, "You've never forgiven him, have you?"

"Have you?" challenged Katie.

Marge nodded. "A long time ago, right after I came to know the Lord. It was just too painful to hold onto all that hatred I felt for Kenneth."

Stunned, Katie realized it had been years since they'd even spoken his name. Slowly she said, "Why didn't you ever talk about…about things?"

"I should have. I can see that I've failed you badly. But you didn't seem to want me to, and I was cowardly. I didn't want you hurt anymore." She sighed. "Whatever reasons I thought I had, they were wrong."

Katie reached out and grasped her mother's hand tightly, remembering how Marge had always tried to protect her. "What did you mean when you said that Will is like him?"

"You were fourteen when Kenneth left, Katie, old enough to remember how alive, how marvelously intense he is. He could walk into a room and the atmosphere would change, almost crackle. People would perk up, get brighter, start talking louder, even. Just Kenneth's presence affected them."

It was hard to see her mother's face in the darkness, but Katie tried. "Mom, it sounds as though you still care. How could you?"

Marge shook her head. "I don't know. Part of me hated him with the most awful desperation I thought I'd die, and part of me still loved him so much I thought I'd…die."

"I'm so sorry—it was horrible for you, and I was off in my private fog!" Katie dropped to her knees beside her mother. "Is that why you never go out, never seem interested in marrying again? Do you still love him?"

The answer didn't come immediately. And when it did Katie had to lean close to hear. "I suppose, in a way. He was the first man to waken passion in me, Katie, and we loved each other so much."

The thought came to Katie of her own new emotions, the ones Will had roused in her that surprised her so with their intensity. "What happened, Mom, what went wrong?"

"Oh, Katie, I could blame it on so many things. But when I look back now I realize there was just one that Kenneth and I couldn't overcome."

"His infidelity?" The small, brave question nearly choked Katie.

"No, Katie. That would never have happened if we hadn't been so selfish, both of us. Neither of us ever learned that real love puts the welfare of the other person above his own. I insisted on my rights, he insisted on his. There was never anything major, just a series of unimportant stalemates until we both withdrew. Only he withdrew into someone else's bed."

"But you weren't wrong to reject him after that!"

Marge shrugged, evidently not wanting to comment on Katie's impassioned statement. And what she did say was puzzling at first. "Katie, you mustn't settle for second best."

"What do you mean?"

"Just that before everything came apart Kenneth and I had almost everything, and we were as happy as it's possible to be, outside a Christian marriage." She paused, a look of such regret on her face it made Katie's heart turn over. Before she could say anything, however, Marge went on resolutely. "I want you to have it all...a Christian marriage with a man who loves God and will cherish you. And..."

"What, Mom?" Katie prompted softly.

Marge met her daughter's eyes squarely, and it was plain that although she felt she might be interfering, she had to say it. "I've come to feel you'd be better off alone, like me, if there's no passion in your relationship."

Katie felt a guilty nudge as she thought of how detached she felt when Justin kissed her. "But what about respect, and gentleness, and kindness, and patience—"

"All those things Justin shows?"

"Yes, as a matter of fact!"

"Isn't Will Adams respectful, and gentle, and kind, and patient, and, ahem...passionate?" She made a funny little sound in the darkness.

"Mother, are you laughing at me?"

She didn't deny or confirm that. "Answer my question."

"Oh, yes, he is."

"How does he feel about you?"

"I...I'm not sure."

"Aren't you now," she said drily, then added, "he cares a great deal."

"Do you really think so?" The words were hesitant, almost pitiful sounding.

"Kathleen Leah Holland, grow up!"

Katie tried hard to be offended at her mother's words, then started to laugh instead. "I guess it's about time, isn't it!"

"At almost twenty-five, I'd say it definitely is. Let's go inside and have a cup of tea. After all this soul-baring I'm thirsty."

In the warm kitchen a few minutes later, hands clasping the warmth of her favorite blue mug, Marge sat on the stool opposite her daughter at the island. Katie was saying, "Mom, I know it hasn't been easy for you, dragging all this up. But I'd like to know one more thing."

"I'll try." She smiled, making Katie wonder again what her father had ever seen in the Barbie doll. Marge

Holland was a very attractive woman, even a daughter could see that. "Do you still feel as though you are married to him? Is that why you haven't married again?"

Marge shook her head. "No, Katie. He broke the relationship—what the two of us shared—when he had sex with that young woman."

"But you said you still loved him then, that you do now."

"It takes more than love, Katie, more than passion, as important as they both are." She finished her tea, then went to the sink to rinse the mug, her back to Katie.

There seemed to be a look of sadness even in the slump of her shoulders. Katie knew she might be pushing into forbidden territory, but she had to know. "Mom, would you have gone back to him?"

Not turning around, Marge said softly, "I'm not sure what I would have done. But I've searched the Bible for myself and prayed about it. The one strong conclusion that I've come to is that if he had asked, and if I had been willing, God could have healed all the wounds, made us one again." Marge turned now, and faced Katie. "But he never asked, and I'll never know for sure what I would have done."

Katie saw the grief on her face, knew her mother had revealed far more than she wanted to. "Mom, I'm sorry to rake all this up, and on your birthday. I know you'd probably rather not talk about it."

"That's not so, Katie. If it helps you to clarify your mind, then it's worth whatever it costs me. I want what's best for you, you know that."

A grin lurked at the corners of Katie's mouth. "If that isn't a statement to make me want to grow up, I've never heard one!" She went to Marge and put her arms around her, and held on tight. "Happy birthday, and thanks, Mom."

Marge's head only reached Katie's shoulder, and her words were muffled against her daughter's sweater. "How many times have I heard that—whether it was for a peanut butter sandwich or lessons on life—'thanks, Mom.'"

"I really mean it. Thanks for being my mom. I wish thinks could have been different for you."

"Just so they are for you, Katie, just so they are for you."

Chapter Nine

Sharon wasn't in the apartment when Katie arrived late Sunday night. She was grateful to be able to take a long hot soak in the tub and climb wearily into bed without having to explain the weekend that had just passed. Explain it? How could she explain it even to herself? She punched her flabby pillow, but those poor feathers had about had it. Too many adolescent tears had soaked them, disintegrated them. She had never cried adolescent tears about boys—those tears had been for her mother, and for herself in the long days and months after her father left. She hadn't allowed herself to think of Kenneth Holland in a very long time, but he came vibrantly to her mind now.

Tall, with hair which was darker and thicker than Katie's own. Eyes that changed according to his mood; green when he was happy, which was most of the time, and sort of a golden green-brown when he was angry, which was seldom, but awesome. Katie had many warm memories of her father that she had successfully blocked out. They came rushing back now.

Picnics on the beach—he loved fried chicken. The way he laughed. He was always laughing, said it kept him young. Once when he and Katie and her mother were on a long walk on the beach he had made a startling, confusing comment. "I'm not going to get old,

Katie-girl. Your mom is, but I'm going to get younger and younger until I'm a baby and I can start the whole glorious thing over again!"

Katie wasn't old enough to understand then, and she'd shoved the remark far to the back of her mind. Her father had been obsessed with the fear of growing old so much that he simply had never grown up, and his obsession had nearly ruined them all. She felt the old burning anger again. How could he have been so selfish, so childish? All the good memories fled and she spent the remainder of the long restless night trying to sleep, aware that her father wasn't the only one who had made a mess of things. Her life was thoroughly confused, too, and somehow she blamed him.

If he hadn't left, things would have been different. She wouldn't have been so withdrawn and distrustful, or waited until she was almost through high school to date. After those first few attempts, disastrous because of her uncertainty, she acquired the reputation of being an ice-maiden. She had become afraid to go out. Justin, with his patient, quiet way of not letting go of her, had been the first man she dated more than once or twice.

Katie had tried to convince herself Justin was the kind of man she wanted, and needed—until Will came along. Will, with all that intense fire in him; Will, who could be as gentle and patient and persistent with his kids as Justin was with her. Katie had the uneasy feeling Will wouldn't be the same with her, that he would leave her alone until she made up her own mind.

She tried hard to sort out her muddled feelings, but the only thing that emerged clearly after that night was that she must somehow tell Justin she couldn't marry him. She would have to tell him Saturday night.

The enormity of that task sunk in over a breakfast which Sharon had waiting when Katie finally left her bedroom Monday morning. Sharon demanded to hear about the weekend. "Tell me everything! Justin called here Friday afternoon—must have been right after you left—and said he planned to drive down to your mother's and surprise you."

Katie sipped her orange juice and smiled in spite of her sleepless-night feeling at the sight of Sharon in her favorite sleeping outfit—a University of Washington football jersey which came to her knees. "Oh, Sharon, he surprised me all right. And he almost proposed—"

"What? When was this?"

Katie sighed. "Right after Will kissed me."

Sharon's big gray eyes got even bigger as she said in a dramatically hushed voice, "Wait. You mean to tell me Will kissed you in the middle of an almost-proposal from Justin?"

"Not exactly, but Sharon, it's such a mess."

"I can see that," said Sharon in delighted horror. "Start at the beginning, roomie." She sat cross-legged on the chair and listened with her whole self, as usual.

"...And the crazy evening ended with Mom telling me some things about her and Dad that I'm still having trouble sorting out," finished Katie quite a bit later.

Sharon, a wrinkle between her brows, said slowly, "Now let me get this straight. Justin promised to propose next Saturday night, but you're going to refuse because you've discovered you're in love with Will Adams?"

Katie couldn't help letting out a plaintive moan. "It sounds even worse when you say it. How *could* I have been so stupid?" She didn't really expect an answer, even from Sharon, and went on slowly, "I don't know if I'm truly in love with Will, I only know I don't want to marry Justin."

"I could have told you that," muttered Sharon. "Well, what are you going to do now? Besides finish your breakfast, that is. I don't get up and do this every day, you know."

Dutifully Katie took a bite of the french toast which was surprisingly good, and she said so. "How do you make it?"

"It's my own recipe. See, I just put a sprinkle of cinnamon and vanilla in with the milk and egg—" She narrowed her eyes. "Hey, you're trying to put me off. You didn't answer my question. What next? Or maybe you don't want to tell me."

"Oh, Sharon, it's not that. It's just that I'm not sure what I should do. Justin is going to be out of town all week, so I can't talk to him until Saturday."

"That breaks your heart, I'll bet," Sharon said, not bothering to keep the sarcasm out of her voice.

Katie bit her lip. "Don't rub it in. You know I'd just as soon never have to face him."

"You will, and he'll be fine. Computer Men don't bleed," she said a little callously. "The big question is what do you do about Will?"

"What can I do? He never said he loved me, and I don't know exactly how I feel about him."

"But you sure would like to find out, wouldn't you?" was her sage comment. "They tell me that's the fun part, finding out."

Katie's nod was slight, but plain. "It's ridiculous, a woman my age getting herself into a predicament like this."

Cheerfully Sharon said, "Hey, you're just a late bloomer, roomie."

"That's what Will says…"

"He does, huh?" Sharon's gap-toothed grin showed her delight. "My advice is to get yourself to school and let the teacher finish your education."

Her expression was so naughty and suggestive that Katie threw a napkin at her, but she finished her french toast, suddenly in a great hurry to do just what Sharon said. The thought of Justin and Saturday night still lurked in the back of her mind, but she pushed it aside.

Katie didn't know what to expect from Will, but his manner when she arrived at the preschool was so very much like that first day when they met she was disheartened. He carefully, politely went over some changes in Eddie's program, asked her if she understood them, and then went about his own business for the next hour or so, not paying her much attention at all.

She tried not to let his distant attitude interfere with her concentration, but she was halfway through Eddie's program before she succeeded. Eddie was a delightful child who never seemed to be unhappy. Physically he was close to beautiful. His hair was soft and brown and curly; his eyes were merry and brown. She often teased him about that dimple close to the right side of his ever-smiling mouth. How many times had Katie hugged him close and wished his brain could be like his disposition—perfect?

He chuckled now as she said, for the sixth time, "No, Eddie, you must show me your shirt, not your pants. Let's start again."

Katie didn't lack patience, but she was always caught off-guard by the occasional sudden blankness in Eddie's eyes. It was gone so quickly she tried to convince herself she hadn't seen it. But it was there from time to time, puzzling and disturbing, and not even Will could explain why. Something wrong in his brain, probably caused at birth, was his only explanation. But that something prevented Eddie from completing tasks and learning in a progressive way.

She sighed and touched his chubby belly. "Let's try again, Eddie. This is your shirt." She knew the sequence by heart now: *Phase I, child will show article of clothing, with complete assistance from adult. Phase II, child will show article of clothing with adult placing child's hand on the clothing, with child maintaining grasp. Phase III, child will show article of clothing with adult touching child's clothes, child imitates. Phase IV, child will show article of clothing when asked.* It seemed so simple. But somehow Eddie couldn't grasp it. Finally she marked Phase II and hugged him before she lifted him from the chair.

"Pooh?" he asked, flashing a dimpled grin.

She nodded, because Will had given her no more instructions and Stacy was not at school today. She couldn't bring herself to ask him after his earlier coolness, but her eyes kept straying to Will's tall figure while she was reading to Eddie.

By the time all the children had been collected and cleanup was completed, Katie had made up her mind. She had to talk to him—but not here or now. Somehow she couldn't just ask him, so she formulated a rather vague plan of going by his apartment, when she felt courageous enough. Well aware that she was acting like a schoolgirl, she smiled and waved good-bye to him, her mind teeming with schemes and plans.

The plan she finally decided on included a picnic basket laden with chicken from the deli (she'd never learned to fry it without burning it), potato salad which her mother had taught her to do passably well, a plastic container of crisp vegetables, and chocolate chip cookies. Of all the ridiculous urges that had ever presented themselves to her, she wondered at giving in to this one. Softening Will up with Toll House cookies was just too much like a smitten cheerleader trying to interest the football captain.

Too late now, she told herself after she'd rung his doorbell, *Unless he wasn't home*. She turned quickly to go, then the door opened behind her.

"Katie?" She heard the questioning in his voice even before she turned back. And it was also in his face. "Do you often go on picnics at night?" he asked.

She took a deep breath and said quickly, "Only when I have a huge apology to make and I would have made it earlier—only I burned the chicken and had to go to the deli to get some more and—"

"Whoa!" He laughed. "Why don't you come on in, this might take a while."

"I'd rather you came to the park with me."

"Well, I have a lot of work to do." His face had that

wary look again. "Katie, it might be best if we let this be. I was mighty uncomfortable on the beach the other night."

"I know." Katie shifted the silly basket from one hand to the other nervously, thinking the whole thing was really uncomfortable now, but determined to see it through. "Will, please, let's at least talk about it."

"I'm not sure it'll do much good," he said gravely.

"Please?" She looked shamelessly up into those blue eyes, beseeching with her own. Suddenly he grinned, and Katie felt a great surge of relief, and hope, and just plain happiness.

"Now how can a man resist that? Do you have time for me to get my shoes, or should I just go barefoot?"

"I'll wait for you."

It was only a few moments later that he came out, shoes and socks in hand, and flopped on the grass outside the apartment building. Katie watched him pull on his socks and lace his jogging shoes with the same intensity he did everything...especially kissing. She shook her head to be rid of that disturbing thought as he stood and said, "Do you trust me with the precious basket? I should warn you that all I had for lunch was a bowl of cornflakes, but I'll do my best to wait."

She handed it over and was content to stroll beside him in silence. It was the end of a perfect day as far as the weather was concerned, the kind of day which called people out of their homes. Dads and kids were playing catch, moms were sitting on steps watching and putting off going inside, bicycles and trikes and children were everywhere. The very air smelled of summer—not flowers now, but outdoor barbeque. Someone had thought of it, and the pungent, evocative aroma had evidently started an epidemic, because it was very strong.

"Barbeque," murmured Will.

"Uh huh," said Katie. "I like the smell of a fire on the beach better." That thought brought to mind the scene on the beach Friday night, so she said hastily, "We're almost to the park. Ever been there?"

He shook his head. "No, not yet."

His quiet, non-committal words made her wonder again if she had made a mistake. "You think I'm childish, don't you?"

"Of course not. I think it's a great idea, and besides, I'm hungry," he said, hearing the anxiety in her voice. "That looks like a good spot." He pointed to a table tucked back under some trees, their tender, spring-green leaves waving a little in the slight breeze which had begun to stir.

Katie laid out the food, glad she'd made a list. She knew better than to undertake anything without one. Blue-checked cloth and napkins, silver, even real glasses for the lemonade. She hated plastic. Aware that Will was watching her as he leaned against the willow tree, she tried to work slowly and not drop anything. From time to time she couldn't keep from glancing at him, and she wished he wasn't watching her so openly, so intently. It made her nervous, or anxious, or…something. What had he said, *"I take you so seriously I convince myself there's no such person as Justin Moore, that you'd be glad if I kissed you."*

Just remembering those words made her face feel warm, although the evening air was beginning to cool. "Ready to eat?" she asked, hoping her voice sounded normal.

"You don't have to ask that question twice," he said, and came over to sit beside her on the bench. After an awkward little silence, he took her hand in his. "At home we all hold hands when we ask the blessing. Is that all right with you?"

She nodded, feeling the warmth of his fingers on her own. She bowed her head and closed her eyes, asking God's forgiveness very quickly because she was more concerned with her reactions to Will than she was grateful for the food.

His voice was deep and quiet as he began, "Father God, we thank you for the day we've had and for...friends. Be with us now as we share this food, and help us to be honest as we share ourselves. In Jesus' name we pray, Amen."

"Amen," breathed Katie, curiously aware that she had never prayed privately with a man before. Her father was not a Christian, and somehow Justin rarely brought up the subject. Curious.

Will more than made up for her lack of appetite. On his fourth piece of chicken he grinned and said, "It may look like it, but I don't plan to eat the whole chicken. Aren't you hungry?"

"Not much. Must be more spring fever."

"Maybe." He noticed the chocolate chip cookies and ate his way through a half dozen with his third glass of lemonade before he said matter-of-factly, "More likely it's what happened the other night on the beach that's bothering you."

She nodded. "Will, I'm so sorry it happened that way. You must think I'm terrible."

"That's not what I think at all."

Katie's throat clogged suddenly. "I acted like such an idiot when you kissed me, but I couldn't help it. I'd never felt like that before."

"That's good," he said huskily.

"But I can't explain it, and I need to be able to!"

He was sitting very close on the wooden bench, and he turned slightly to face her. The moon was rising, and it shone softly through the hanging fluff of high clouds, through the lacy willow leaves onto her face. "If I kissed you again, would it help, do you think?" His voice was light, teasing, and heartstoppingly serious at the same time.

"Will, I..." Suddenly his arms were tight around her and when his lips met hers she could only moan a little. It was the same as before, only more devastating. For a long, floating moment afterwards, she didn't even try to speak. There were no words; none were needed. Finally she whispered, "I think...I think I must be falling in love with you."

He laughed. "You see? I told you another kiss would help you figure things out. There's no telling what a couple more would do."

She didn't protest. She neither wanted to, nor could she have if she *had* wanted to. His mouth found hers again, explored its sweet softness, made her forget everything but the fire in her blood. Only now she wasn't afraid or confused, just full of the most wonderful, exciting sensations imaginable.

"Oh, Katie," he murmured reluctantly, "one of us has got to blow the whistle."

She felt a giggle as she remembered Sharon's words about finishing her education. She managed to stifle her laughter, but couldn't keep from saying, "You're the teacher..."

"So I am, and you're the best pupil I ever had! Well, time out, before I forget I'm a Christian gentleman."

"You wouldn't, right here in public?" she teased.

"Don't count on it, not unless I move myself completely away from temptation," he said lightly. But he did get up and go around the table, seating himself opposite her. "There, I feel safer."

"You sound like I'm a menace."

"Just about the truth. Umbrellas in the nose, cold shoulders on the beach, midnight picnics—"

"It's not even nine o'clock," she protested softly, enjoying the banter. She and Justin never teased each other, never acted silly. Justin. The thought of him sobered her immediately.

Will's face mirrored her feelings. "I'll bet I can guess what you're thinking about. Justin?"

She nodded. "We've dated for so long, and he has always believed if he gave me enough time I'd..."

"Love him?" supplied Will quietly. "But you don't, do you, Katie?"

"No, I've been so selfish, Will; selfish and immature." She bowed her head and said, her voice low, "And now he thinks I'm willing to marry him."

"Why would he think that?"

Katie was suddenly cold, not certain the feeling was caused by the stirring breeze or the sharp sound in Will's voice. "Because when he talked about it the other night I didn't say no."

"The other night after I left."

"Yes. But, Will, I didn't say yes, either. I was confused, and he's been a part of my life for such a long time, and he has always made me feel safe—" She choked, and couldn't go any further.

Thoughtfully Will said, "Safe. Poor Justin. Did you let him kiss you, and hold you?"

"Yes, but—"

"You had quite a night, it seems to me. So Justin did me one better and proposed?" She nodded miserably. "And you just couldn't make up your mind. Does he know that there seems to be a contest? Or have you told him?"

She could only shake her head; she didn't know what to say. Baldly stated like that it did sound cowardly, and worse, made her seem calculating and heartless. It wasn't exactly true, but she'd have bitten her tongue off before she tried to defend herself.

Will was silent for a long, painful time. Then he rose and put the food and dishes back into the basket carefully, methodically. "I'll walk you home, Katie. You shouldn't be walking alone at night."

"Please, Will, you aren't going to leave it like this, are you?"

"There's nothing else I can do," he said heavily. "You've been playing games with both of us. Can you tell me I'm wrong?"

"No," she whispered. Hadn't she thought so herself, in a way?

"Only once—that concert, did I break down and ask

you out, and even then I couldn't help but think I was being unfair to Justin. I didn't want to interfere or cause any trouble between you. But the other night on the beach...and just a while ago, you seemed to want me as much as I did you."

"Oh, Will, I did."

He shook his head, as if to clear it. "I guess I assumed you'd break it off with him. The poor guy."

Suddenly Katie was angry, and she latched onto the feeling like a drowning man would a life preserver. Never mind that Will was right, never mind that he was telling the truth, that she should have told Justin right there on the beach she didn't intend to marry him. At that moment she only saw them all lined against her in their maleness—her father, Justin, and Will.

"That's typical, for you to side with Justin! Don't you feel any responsibility at all?"

"That's a good word, Katie. As soon as you figure out what it means, let me know. Until then, leave me out of your little games. I'm too old for them. I need a woman, not a girl who doesn't know her mind, or her heart."

Katie was more confused than ever, and angry and hurt as well. She could think of nothing to say on the short walk to her house that wouldn't make things worse. Because the only words that came to her tongue were sharp, bitter, and mostly untrue. Will left her at her door after a polite good-bye, and she crept inside, grateful that at least she was still dry-eyed.

Chapter Ten

If time had flown before for Katie, it dragged on wings of iron now, like that sculptured eagle in Will's apartment. Saturday seemed light years away. It wasn't as though she was looking forward to having dinner with Justin—her mind skittered away from that image every time it crept near. How do you tell a man that for almost two years you've been playing a game? Katie tried to defend her actions by telling herself she'd never actually—until last Friday night, that is—told Justin she loved him.

But in her heart she knew very well she had let him believe she did love him, or was growing to. Clearly most of the fault lay with her. She slept badly, and more often than not ended up on her knees by the side of her bed. Even here there was no comfort, and for the first time since she'd become a Christian she began to doubt her relationship with God. She longed to talk to Will about it, and couldn't, of course. The polite distance between them couldn't be spanned by a hundred bridges.

On Thursday evening in desperation she found herself turning the pages of her Bible, feeling foolishly like the heroine in a B-western movie who dramatically opens the big family Bible and, eyes closed, places her pretty finger on The Answer.

It wasn't so easy for Katie. There was no answer, until a tiny, whispering memory came repeatedly, softly to the edge of her consciousness. *Forgive.* She stared at the printed words in her Bible until they seemed to jump about on the page. *Forgive.* What had Will said? God doesn't withhold forgiveness because we've been bad, or sinful. We shut the door between us and Him when we refuse to forgive others.

Suddenly she felt a faint stirring of hope and turned quickly to the concordance of her Bible. *Forgive.* She leafed back to the sixth chapter of Matthew and found the familiar words.

Our Father, who art in heaven,
Hallowed be Thy name.
Thy kingdom come.
Thy will be done,
On earth as it is in heaven.
Give us this day our daily bread.
And forgive us our debts, as we also
  have forgiven our debtors.
And do not lead us into temptation,
  but deliver us from evil.
For thine is the kingdom, and the power,
  and the glory, forever. Amen.
For if you forgive men for their transgressions, your heavenly Father will also forgive you. But if you do not forgive men, then your Father will not forgive your transgressions.

Katie stared at the words, realizing suddenly that although she had learned them as a child, had heard them spoken and sung in church and at weddings, they had never truly been a part of her. It was like the faint light at the end of a long black tunnel, but light it was, even when she closed her eyes and whispered, "Oh, Father, forgive me..."

It was the beginning of a careful, far-reaching process. The search led from Mr. Van Pelt and his pale wife with her haunted eyes and twisting hands to a face Katie had tried to forget—her father's face, so like her own...wide-spaced green eyes, a mouth that laughed easily and made extravagant promises. Promises that were shattered and never renewed, an idol broken forever. But he was still her father, and she needed to forgive him.

When Katie emerged from her room the next morning Sharon sensed something different about her friend. She did not greet her with the same sassiness she had used every other morning that week in an effort to cheer Katie up. She merely said, quietly for Sharon, "You look like you slept for the first time this week."

Katie nodded, a tremulous smile on her lips. "I did, and I can't tell you how much better I feel."

"Well, Justin will be home tomorrow. Are you...do you think you'll be—" For once she seemed at a loss for words.

But Katie, glass of juice in hand as she looked out the window at the brilliant new day, said softly, "I think so. It won't be easy, but I have to face him. I have to tell him the truth."

"Which is?"

"That I don't love him in the way he needs, and can't ever," Katie said simply. "That I'm very, very sorry for having led him on—"

"You're not going to tell him *that*?" Sharon yelped.

"It's true, Sharon."

"But you didn't mean to! I know you, Katie, and I know you wouldn't do that deliberately."

"The bottom line is, I did it. I'm not a child, and I can't go on acting childishly. I've got to get started growing up." She sighed, that little smile on her lips again. "That's what Mom told me, and so did he."

"Who, Justin?"

Katie shook her head. "Will. He's the one who said I

was playing games and that he was too old for games."

"Are you sure he isn't just playing games with your head?" she asked suspiciously. As always, Sharon sided with her friend. She was nothing if not loyal.

The sun shining through the multi-paned windows made bright squares on the toast-colored carpet. Katie stared at them for a long while. "No, Will's not playing games at all. He's one of the few people I've ever known who's just what he seems to be."

Sharon grinned. "And you're head over heels in love with him, aren't you?"

"Yes," said Katie slowly, as if she couldn't quite take in the fact herself, "I am."

"Wonderful!" crowed Sharon. "When do you think he'll pop the question?"

Katie's laughter rang out and seemed to mix with the bright sunlight. "The only one who's mentioned marriage is Justin." She sobered suddenly at the thought. There was nothing at all funny in the situation with Justin and he deserved better. She also realized something else and said slowly, "And Will may never propose to me. I don't know if I'm the kind of woman he needs, Sharon."

"Are you saying he might not think you're good enough for him?" Sharon asked fiercely. "Because if he doesn't, *I'll* have a talk with him!"

"No, no, I didn't mean that at all. If anyone doesn't think I'm good enough, it's me. Will deserves a special woman."

"You're special," grumbled Sharon, sensing that Katie had finished with the discussion and was not going to pursue it any further.

She was right. Absently Katie finished her juice, put the glass in the dishwasher, and went about getting ready for school, all the time with that peculiar, different look on her face. Sharon thought it was almost as though the sun streaming in the windows had touched her friend's face and stayed there.

As Katie left for her early class, Sharon called out the tattered, familiar phrase, "Have a good day, roomie," and Katie's reply floated back.

"Thanks, Sharon, I will…"

Katie's first class went well, and it looked as though the overused but sincerely spoken words might be prophetic today. At least she thought so until she arrived at the preschool. There was a disturbing undercurrent in the air that she couldn't place.

She looked for Will, but he was nowhere in sight. She didn't know whether she was relieved or disappointed. His meticulously polite, distant attitude hadn't changed all week except for those few moments of closeness in the park Monday night. Katie couldn't fault him. She understood he'd probably decided it was the best way to handle the situation, especially since they had to work together.

Besides, she hadn't had an opportunity on Monday evening to tell him Justin was out of town, and she didn't feel like reopening the whole thing until she had faced Justin. So she had mirrored Will's distant politeness, wondering if he were trying to suppress completely or even rid himself entirely of what he felt for her.

After wandering distractedly around the playroom for a while, picking up first Robby, then Mark, then taking Stacy from his Infanseat, she decided there was something else wrong. Finally she saw Ellen coming from the room where the staff did most of the work with the children's programs, Julie in tow.

"Come on, sweetie, you did great today," she was saying to the child, whose thin little face was angelically pleased at Ellen's praise.

The expression on Ellen's face made up Katie's mind. With Stacy on her hip, she went over to Ellen. "Would you please tell me what's going on? The very air around here is thick with something!"

Ellen stared at her. "You mean Will didn't tell you?"

"I haven't seen him yet." A stab of panic hit Katie's stomach. "What's happened?"

Ellen took Katie's arm, and with her other hand led Julie to the clothes basket filled with toys. "Come over here and sit down, huh?"

Katie thought perhaps the sound of her heart beating in sudden fear might be audible. She allowed Ellen to steer her to the rocking chair where she sat holding Stacy close in her arms as she stared into Ellen's drawn face. "One of the children?" Ellen nodded, her lip caught in her teeth. Katie looked around the room, her eyes seeing each child, her mind ticking off each one. Slowly, she asked, "It's Eddie, isn't it?"

"Yes, Katie. His grandmother called a little while ago. He died last night. I'm sorry. I know how you loved him." Her face was soft with compassion.

"He died?" Katie made a funny little choking sound and felt the sting of tears. "But he was so beautiful, so healthy looking."

"It was an epileptic seizure in his sleep. He never woke up, Katie, so there probably wasn't any pain at all."

"No pain," Katie whispered, feeling the knife thrust of pain herself at the thought of never again seeing Eddie; his bright eyes and ruddy cheeks with that dimple, his roguish, deep belly chuckles at Pooh's antics. The warm tears slid quietly down Katie's cheeks onto Stacy's downy head. He didn't notice, for he'd fallen asleep. Katie rocked him gently, placing a kiss on his forehead every so often.

Ellen didn't say much more, but she sat close to Katie until Will came into the room and noticed the silent tears. Then she slipped away as he came and bent over Katie.

"Honey, I know you loved him too," he murmured. "I should have been the one to tell you, I'm sorry."

She nodded, not able to speak, and he put his hand on her neck, warm and comforting. "We'll talk about it after the kids leave if you want." Once again she only nodded, and he stood for a while longer, then gave her neck a light squeeze as if to say, I know, I know. He went on about his usual business with the other children, almost as though it were any normal day.

But it was far from being like any other day. The children were very sensitive to the emotion-charged atmosphere. Some reacted by becoming very quiet and subdued. Stacy was one of these. He clung to Katie, whimpering softly if she tried to put him down. Others, Julie in particular, were agitated to the point of frenzy. Today she wasn't biting, she just pulled hair whenever she could get a handful. After the third time Will signaled Ellen to keep a close eye on Julie, and he went to call the parents, explaining the circumstances and suggesting they pick up their children early.

When the children were all gone Will gathered the staff together. They sat in the low chairs around the children's table, the same stricken look on each face, listening as Will, his voice low and controlled, spoke of Eddie. Katie listened too, still feeling dazed, but it was his last few words that caught her attention.

"We'll all miss Eddie, mostly because he was a happy little boy who made us feel happy too. His was a bright spirit and he taught me a lot..."

Katie had been staring out the window but she looked now at Will's face. It was composed, calm, but she felt the pain in his voice, saw it in his eyes. Whether or not the others were as aware of it she didn't know. One by one they wandered out, not speaking much. When only Katie and Will remained in the now quiet, sunny room, his eyes met hers.

"Will, I—" she began, then stopped suddenly, for the words clogged in her throat.

He nodded, and she knew he understood. "Want to drive over to the beach?"

The thought of walking on the beach right now was

such a welcome one that she cried, "Oh, that's a wonderful idea!"

A faint smile that didn't reach his eyes curved his mouth. "I remember what you said about how it heals." He went over and took his windbreaker from the coatrack, but he stood there staring for so long, a stricken look on his face, that Katie came over to him. There, next to the hook with Will's name on it was Eddie's name, and a red cap, forgotten on another day, hung beneath it.

"He liked red," was all Will said.

Katie touched his arm gently, and finally they walked out of the room together, her arm linked in his.

In the hour it took to reach the ocean neither Will nor Katie spoke much, but it was a silence of shared emotion and not uncomfortable. Contrary to Katie's weather adage of clear inland, stormy on the beach, the sun sparkled on a calm, blue sea. They walked facing a salty breeze past Spanish Head, past the driftwood beach at Boiler Bay, almost to the bridge over the creek that was wild and rushing with spring run-off.

For Katie, who had always relied on the thunder of the surf and the sea winds to clear her mind of whatever troubled her, it worked. She felt calmer. But there were still so many unanswered questions. Will walked over to a massive log that had been thrown ashore by rough seas a month ago, deposited close to the sandy cliff, and not touched by the water since. He sat on its wind and sun-dried silvery surface and Katie sat beside him.

"I can see you're a little better." He looked closely at her. "Tell me what you're thinking, honey."

Katie's eyes filled with tears at the low, tender sound of his words. "I just don't understand."

"You mean why Eddie had to die."

She nodded numbly. "And when you were talking about how happy he always was I couldn't help but think how unfair it is that his life was cut short. He enjoyed everything so much…"

"It does seem unfair, doesn't it," he agreed, his voice quiet. He stared out at the water for a long while. The tide was ebbing, and waves lapped farther away each time, leaving an uneven pattern of bubbly foam all along the sand. Little shore birds, their long, thin legs moving with amazing rapidity, darted back and forth, gleaning from the harvest left at the water's line.

"Why, Will," Katie said finally, "why did it happen?"

He looked into her eyes. "Katie, you sound as though you think if there were an answer, I'd know it."

She didn't flinch at the question in his eyes or in his voice. "It's just that I trust you, Will. If you do have an answer, I know you would only have found it through a lot of searching."

"You seem to have more faith in me than I have in myself," he said, running his fingers through his hair.

"I trust you," she repeated quietly, wondering at her attitude toward Will. It hadn't been so long ago she had first realized how much Justin was responsible for shaping her thoughts and opinions, and had begun to resist, even resent his subtle control. And here she was asking for the same thing from Will. *No,* something deep within her whispered, *it's not the same at all.*

For a long while he continued to gaze into her eyes, as though he himself were searching for something. At last he said, "I hope you aren't disappointed in me, Katie. But the only answer I have is a simple one. I guess I just believe Eddie had a brain that didn't always function properly, and last night a seizure caused his little body to stop breathing. It happened because of something that occurred when he was born, something that damaged his brain."

"But...are you saying God didn't have anything to do with it?" Katie expected him to say something far different; she felt more confused than ever.

"No, I didn't mean to imply that at all. God has everything to do with it."

She shook her head. "I don't understand."

"And I may not be able to help you understand, for all that trust you have in me."

He looked so grave, so hesitant, that she briefly touched his wind-cool cheek. "Try, Will, try."

He took a deep breath, then began again. "I believe with all my heart that God is in control of His world, and nothing happens that He is not aware of, that He doesn't care about. But we're not puppets, on holy strings. He allows us to do things against His will, and things happen to us, to our bodies, that make Him as sorrowful, or more, than they do us."

"Then you believe that God grieves for Eddie's trouble, just like we do?"

"Yes, I know He does. When you care, and love, you grieve."

"And I know God loves Eddie, and that Eddie is with Him in a different way now." Katie sighed softly.

"No more seizures, no more problems." Will's voice was gentle and low.

"But why does it have to hurt this much?" she whispered. "Eddie was so dear." She thought perhaps the freshening south wind had snatched her words away. Will didn't answer for a long time.

"Remember what we talked about after you saw that painting at my place? That we learn the most from the most difficult times?"

"Yes...but it's so hard."

He put his arms around her and she laid her head on the smooth nylon of his windbreaker. "I know, honey, I know."

Katie felt the depth of his understanding and was comforted by his touch. When by mutual silent agreement they rose from the log and began the long walk back, it was hand in hand, companionably close.

As he was backing his truck out of the parking lot, Will glanced over at her. "Would you mind not stopping by your mother's?"

"No, of course not. I hadn't thought of it, to tell the truth."

"I feel I should get back and see Eddie's parents."

Katie savored the last glimpse of the water; she always felt a small wrench at leaving it. When they turned onto the highway she asked, "Would you like me to go with you?"

"How do you feel about it?" He didn't look at her as he concentrated on maneuvering through the late afternoon traffic.

But Katie was beginning to be able to sense things unsaid in his voice. "You'd like for me to, wouldn't you?"

"Yes, I would, if it wouldn't disturb you too much."

"Then of course I will." Somehow her own reluctance to face Eddie's grieving parents faded before Will's need of her.

The house where Eddie Davis had spent most of his brief life was a modest one. His father, a tall, thin man who had dark eyes which bore the signs of contained tears, answered the door and showed them into the quiet, darkened livingroom.

"Who is it, Ed?" A woman who had been lying on the couch sat up as they entered, her face pale but dry.

"It's Mr. Adams, Eddie's teacher," said her husband, moving slowly as he turned on the lamps.

The woman's face lightened a bit as she saw Katie. "And Katie, isn't it?"

Katie nodded and smiled uncertainly, searching for the right words. None came. For a moment she felt that overwhelming reluctance again, as she had at the thought of coming here. Nothing in her experience had prepared her for this. But at the touch of Will's fingers on her shoulder she went to sit beside the woman and put her arms around her. "I loved him too," was all she was able to whisper.

Mrs. Davis nodded mutely. She leaned slightly against Katie, who marveled at the simple rightness of one person's touching another with gentle caring. Her eyes met Will's briefly and she saw something there that made her heart leap. He knew how hard it had been for her to come, and what it meant to her.

When Eddie's mother drew away she smiled at Will. "Do sit down. I don't know where my manners are. Ed, would you make some coffee, please?"

He nodded and excused himself, and when he returned with steaming mugs of coffee all around they sat for the better part of an hour, talking about Eddie and what he'd meant to them. Though Katie could only suppose what their reactions would be later when the shock wore off, they accepted quietly the things Will said now. His words echoed what he and Katie had discussed a short while ago on the beach.

As they stood at the door just before they left, Katie was able to say, "I'm so glad I knew your son, Mrs. Davis." The woman nodded, and this time she held out her hands to Katie, who took them both in her own, then hugged her close for a moment. "We're both here if you need us."

As he had been throughout the visit, Mr. Davis was quiet now. But he thanked them for coming, and his handshake was hard and eloquent.

When Will braked his truck in front of Katie's house they sat quietly, and again Katie was aware of the quality of the silence between them. It seemed right and easy, a good thing altogether. Will had taken her hand in his almost absently as he gazed out at the tree-lined street, and after a while he said, "I can't tell you how much I appreciate your being with me this afternoon, how much it helped."

"I'm glad," said Katie softly. "You've certainly helped me over some rough spots. I owe you."

He made a little sound halfway between a sigh and a laugh. "Who's keeping score? Not me." Another almost-sigh escaped him, and he increased the pressure on her hand slightly. "Katie, I...would it be all right if we prayed together before you go in?"

Wordlessly she nodded. Her eyes met his for a moment before she bowed her head. *That's why I trust him,* she thought suddenly. *It isn't because he's a better man than Justin at all. He just knows that the real answers aren't within himself or in his own strength.* It seemed to be completely natural for him to want to pray with her. Katie was silent and held tightly to his hand as she waited for him to begin.

He didn't say anything for a few moments and when he did his prayer was very short. "Father, we thank you for your presence, for your comfort. I know Eddie is safe with you, and that you love him far more than we were able to. Help us in our weakness, Lord, and when we can't understand things, help us to get through them anyway. Oh, God—we did love him—"

Katie clutched his hand as his voice broke, feeling the depth of his grief. Finally she whispered, "It will get easier, I know it."

He nodded, and a little later she squeezed his hand again, then released it and slid out of the truck. "Thank you, Will," she said, not knowing exactly what she meant, but grateful to him nonetheless. As she watched him drive away she felt the most extraordinary combination of emotions.

Katie was surer than ever that Will Adams was like no other man she'd ever known. His feelings for Eddie and the way he handled them, his concern for Eddie's parents, and most of all, the simple natural way he had included her made a deep impression on her. And though it seemed to have nothing whatever to do with the passion they had shared on the beach last week and in the park, she had the strong conviction that all those feelings were a part of the whole.

Chapter Eleven

Katie rummaged in her closet for perhaps the fourth time, trying to decide what to wear. A glance at her watch told her there wasn't a great deal of time left to make up her mind, because it was after five and Justin was picking her up at a quarter to six. The feeling of panic that had been nipping at her all day threatened to become a full-blown anxiety attack. She reached for the rose paisley dress—and remembered she had worn it to the concert with Will.

His lean, strong face came so vividly to her mind that she withdrew the dress and stood for a few moments clutching it as she allowed that sweet memory, and others, to fill her mind. The music that night had been so magical, so much a part of her discovery of Will that she had often played it since. Not stopping to analyze her motives, she found the tape he'd given her and listened to it as she dressed in the soft, pretty, paisley dress.

She surveyed herself in the mirror and decided the special care she'd spent on her makeup made a difference. Her hair always behaved better when the rainy season slacked off, and the new style she'd treated herself to this morning was definitely good for her face. It was cut and curled now so that all she had to do was wash and let it dry naturally, making a sort of fluffy, brown-gold halo.

It wasn't like her to change her hairstyle without considering it for several weeks, but she had awakened this morning feeling that nagging anxiety, and made the appointment impulsively. Sharon liked it, but Sharon always loved change. Katie touched her hair tentatively, knowing it was bound to bring comments from Justin. She stared at her reflection. He would be here soon and there would come a time when there would be no more talk of whether or not he liked her new hairstyle, of how his week had gone in San Francisco, or hers. She would have to look into his eyes as squarely as she was looking into her own now and tell him she could not marry him.

Tears blurred her vision suddenly at the thought of how difficult that would be. Just then the third movement of the Rodrigo music began, the one that always made her cry. It was such unbearably, hauntingly lonely music. There was something in it that moved her in a deep way she couldn't explain.

Sharon found her seated on her bed a little later, silent slow tears coursing down her face, the music soft and plaintive. "Katie? Are you all right?" When Katie shook her head, Sharon found a tissue and carefully dabbed at the tears. "Hey, if you're not feeling up to snuff I can have Justin leave and call you later—"

"He's here?" Katie's eyes flew to the door in agitation.

"Yep. And you don't have to see him if you don't want to," said Sharon with a fierce, protective look. "I'll tell him you're sick!"

"No, I have to get this over with, Sharon. I have to talk to him. I've been so unfair to him already, I can't put it off any longer."

"You're sure?"

"Yes. Sharon—" She stopped, seeing the look of concern on her roommate's face. "You really are a good friend. Did I ever tell you that?"

For a moment Sharon seemed torn between being embarrassed at Katie's words and wanting to acknowledge how important the friendship was to her, too. At last, slowly, she said with no hint of the joking manner she sometimes affected, "You don't have to tell me, but it makes me feel good to hear it...and I feel the same way about you, Katie."

"We should be open and honest about our feelings. If I had been with Justin I might not be in this pickle now."

"You'll do fine, roomie," said Sharon firmly. "I've got confidence in you."

Katie smiled and took a deep breath. "I think I'm ready to face the music."

"You bet you are." Her old flip self again, Sharon dropped onto Katie's bed and reached for the tape deck. "Speaking of music, is it okay if I turn off this thing? That stuff will make you crazy." In mid-strum John Williams was cut off, and Sharon's face showed relief. "Too bad you don't have any *good* tapes. Oh, well. I'll just stay in here until you leave, okay?"

"But—"

"You don't need me, and Justin sure doesn't. Besides, I'll probably be here when you get home, with tea and sympathy or whatever. Prayer, maybe?" She grinned. Sharon's relationship with God was like herself—unique and unusual at times, but always real.

"Definitely prayer," Katie murmured, and went out alone to meet Justin.

Because he considered himself a connoisseur of fine eating places, there were not many restaurants in the area that Justin and Katie hadn't tried in the past two years. But he had outdone himself this time, in discovering a small, very private restaurant called Cyrano's. It was only large enough for twelve tables, and each was tucked discreetly behind a wall of greenery, a fountain, or in a secluded alcove with only a table for two in it. He'd reserved one of these.

The elaborate meal had a total of six courses, and although Katie valiantly tried to initiate the subject uppermost on her mind, Justin had smoothly maneuvered the conversation to other topics through five courses so far. Finally, Katie gave up, deciding that he most likely had something definite in mind—a scenario he'd written. She chided herself: *That wasn't a kind thought at all, Katie.*

The candles flickered softly, their light practically the only illumination in the intimate little area. The music from a speaker was as soft as the candlelight and deliberately seductive. Fragile-looking gypsophilia and roses, as delicately pink as a baby's cheek, formed the artful arrangement on the table. It was all very, very romantic, but Katie felt as though she were on a perfectly detailed stage set and was acutely uncomfortable instead of being softly wooed. Poor Justin, he had tried so very hard.

"Well, I've told you all about my week. It's your turn now," said Justin, leaning back expectantly. "Your new hairstyle is very becoming, but you look rather tired, Kathleen."

She shrugged, knowing it was true. "It's been an especially difficult week."

"Exams already, or is it something at the preschool?"

Katie studied his face for a moment. From his expression, she decided he actually seemed interested. He'd probably done some thinking and was going to try and take an interest in the school, since it meant so much to her. "Yes, something has hit me hard. One of the children, his name was Eddie, died unexpectedly. He's...he was one of my favorites."

"That's too bad," he murmured. "You say it was unexpected? What happened?"

"It was a seizure of some sort, and he just didn't wake up one morning. He had suffered brain damage at birth."

"You know, Kathleen, it's probably for the best."

Justin's eyes were full of sympathy but somehow Katie knew it was for her, not Eddie. Slowly she asked,

"Justin, if you had a son like Eddie, or one of the others—"

"That's not going to happen," he said firmly. "Kathleen, when we have children they will be quite perfect, I'm sure." The look of resolute firmness that had come over his face made Katie almost believe that by sheer force of will he could prevent it—almost.

She stared at him, knowing he could not help his feelings, but his expression reminded her of someone else. Then she knew. Justin had the same determined set to his jaw that Mr. Van Pelt had worn the day he brought Stacy to the school.

An almost hysterical thought kept running through her mind. Justin's weakness, an imperfection, so to speak, was his inability to tolerate imperfection. She wanted to say, *"Nobody's perfect, Justin, not even you."* But she sensed they could not really communicate any further on the subject and more importantly, there was no need to. They—she and Justin—would never have a child together. Her head had begun to ache slightly, and she knew that the hardest part of the evening was yet to be endured.

Resolutely she began, "Justin, I thought this week would never end. I—"

But he held up his hand, a self-confident smile on his fine mouth as he reached for her hand. "Please, Kathleen, let me say it first. You're right, it has seemed as though it's been forever. I missed you terribly. Right in the middle of a meeting I'd think of you, and my mind would wander off." His thumb was gently moving over her hand, caressing first one finger then another. "I kept imagining this moment, how perfect everything would be. And it is, don't you think?" He glanced around the exquisite room, a pleased expression on his face.

"Yes, it's been a very nice evening," she agreed faintly.

"Not like the last time...on the beach."

Katie felt two things simultaneously: relief that he'd finally broached the subject, and a sharp twinge of anxiety as to how she should proceed now. "No, it isn't. I'm so sorry about all that."

He shook his head. "Let's forget the whole incident, except for one thing. Do you remember when I said I didn't have your ring with me? Well, I have it now." Still holding her left hand, he reached into his pocket and ceremoniously withdrew a small square box, adroitly opened it and removed the ring, a lovely marquise-cut diamond of impressive size.

"I hope you like it."

"Justin, please—"

But somehow, unbelievably, he seemed not to notice that she was on the verge of tears. Or if he did he thought they were tears of happiness, for he said softly, "I love you, and want you to be my—"

"No!" She pulled away and clasped both hands together, holding them in her lap to stop their trembling. "You've got to listen to me." She steeled herself against the shocked look on his face. "I don't love you, Justin."

"What are you saying? Last week you told me—"

"I know, I know. And I do love you, in a way. You're one of the best, finest men I've ever known, but I don't love you in the way you want me to, the way you deserve."

Quietly, carefully, he said, "Kathleen, you know I've been patient. I was so sure if I gave you time to know your heart, that you'd come to feel the way I do about you."

"But I haven't, and I know now that I never can."

"It's Will Adams, isn't it?"

Katie's heart seemed to skip a beat. She saw that if she wanted to, she could say yes—that it was Will who'd come between them. But she realized it would be less than honest. She would never have loved Justin the way he wanted, even if Will had not come into her life. And that was what she haltingly, slowly, told him. He was silent through every difficult word, silent when she finally finished. Ater a long quiet moment Katie said softly, "You've been more kind and patient than any man should have to be, Justin."

"But that isn't enough, is it?" She shook her head miserably. "It's never been enough," he mused. "I should have seen that, I should have known. But I was too involved with the way I felt about you. I didn't even notice or want to know that it was always one-sided. It's not all your fault, you know." He had the ring on his index finger and twirled it absently around and around.

The beautiful diamond winked mockingly at Katie in the candlelight. "I wish you weren't so calm and reasonable!"

"What do you want me to do?" he asked quietly. "Rant and rave, carry on like...like your intense teacher might do, I suppose?"

Katie sighed. "He might, and then again he might not. I don't know that I'm such a good judge of men."

"Are you going to marry him?"

She smiled wanly. "He hasn't asked me. As a matter of fact, he hasn't even said he loves me..." She trailed off, remembering with a pang that she had confessed to Will she was falling in love with him, but he'd certainly made no such declaration.

Justin stared at the ring for a moment, then placed it carefully in its velvet box and slipped it into his pocket. "Wouldn't it be ironic if you don't want me, and he doesn't want you?" Her face showed the sudden dismay his words caused. He hastened to add, "But it won't happen that way. How could he not...want you?"

"Justin, you're so good," she whispered, "you deserve better than me."

Thoughtfully, he said, "Up until last Friday night I really thought we were meant for each other. And when I found myself brooding about you and Will Adams all week, thinking of you in his arms, I kept telling myself you weren't the kind to become involved with someone else secretively. I blamed him entirely."

"You blamed the wrong person, then. I'm the one who invited Will to go with me to Mom's when you were too busy. And—" She stopped. Her voice was so low he had to lean forward to hear as she said, "Will told me I've been playing games with you, and I want—no, I need to ask your forgiveness for that."

He seemed to be more sensitive to her feelings than he had been before. His own voice was very gentle now. "There's no need to forgive you for anything."

"Please, it's important that I admit the truth, and important that you do, too, and forgive me."

"Then, of course, I do."

For the first time since she'd known him, Justin looked forlorn. Katie wanted to tell him he'd find someone much better, but she knew that would not be wise at all. She watched him struggle, master his feelings, and when the maitre d' came, Justin left for a moment with him to settle the check. At the thought of the expense of the evening she felt a stab of guilt, but she remembered how often she had told Justin that she would enjoy something simpler every bit as much, only to have him assure her that he enjoyed taking her to nice places. She'd certainly never expected it of him.

He returned, once more in possession of himself, and the politeness in his manner and tone on the way home reminded her of Will's remoteness all week. She thought that perhaps in her ineptitude she'd lost them both.

The conversation on the shadowed porch at Katie's house was awkwardly polite and painful for them both. She longed to say something that would make the situation easier for Justin.

"Justin, I hope you know how much you…you've meant to me, how much I appreciate—"

"Don't, please." He stood stiffly, a little apart from her. "I know you're just trying to be kind, but somehow it hurts worse than if you were hardhearted and casual."

"I'm sorry, really I am." Her words were low and gentle in the darkness.

"I know you are." He was quiet for a few moments that seemed endless, then he said slowly, "If...you ever need anything, you'll call, won't you? I mean if things don't work out with Adams."

He sounded the same way he'd looked in the restaurant when she asked for his forgiveness—forlorn. Katie reached out and touched his cheek tenderly with the palm of her hand. He grasped it in his own and held it tightly.

"Kathleen, I'm going to miss you a great deal."

"And I'll miss you. I have so much to thank you for, Justin. You know that, don't you?" Katie was honest enough to be able to admit that if she had not allowed it, Justin wouldn't have dominated her. If they had been able to talk frankly and share their deepest feelings their relationship could have been altogether different. And if she hadn't met Will—but she had. She stepped closer and gave in to the impulse to put her arms around him and hold him tight for a brief moment. "Good-bye, Justin."

But he couldn't bring himself to return her embrace. When Katie released him he looked down at her in the dimness and finally said, "Remember, if you ever need me..."

Then he was gone, leaving Katie to wonder sadly if she could have handled the situation any better, only to decide that her major mistakes had been made so long ago and compounded so thoroughly it was a wonder she'd made it through the evening at all. Then, feeling emotionally drained, she slowly climbed the stairs to the apartment.

The phone was ringing. Katie fumbled with her keys in the dim light at the top of the stairs, all the while hearing the insistent clamor. As happened more often than not, the noise stopped just as she opened the door and made a mad dash across the room. The sudden silence was depressing.

"Sharon?" she called out, hoping to see that shaggy head and her bright curious face pop around the corner. No answer. Katie couldn't remember being so terribly lonely, and needing someone to talk to so much since her father had left.

Resolutely she went to her room and hung up her coat, then her dress. She put her shoes and stockings away with precision, put on her gown and robe, brushed her teeth and hair—anything to put off having nothing to do but think. Then, knowing it might not be wise, nonetheless she put the Rodrigo tape on. All too soon Katie found herself huddled on the end of the couch staring into the darkness, the lovely lonely music turned as loud as though Sharon had adjusted the tape-player.

In her mind's eye she saw Eddie, flashing that dimple at her, giggling and crowing over Pooh's woozle hunt, struggling with his program valiantly. She'd never read to him again, *never see him again*. Suddenly she realized that although she'd been resentful at Justin, in a way he was right. Eddie was with the Lord, and how could that not be better for him? Reason told her it was true, and her heart ached anyway.

She tried to imagine losing someone as close as her mother, and shied away from that possibility immediately. Then her father came to mind. What if he had died and was truly beyond her? For a very long time now she had been acting, in a way, as though he were dead. She let herself imagine for the first time how Kenneth Holland must have felt about leaving his only daughter, his only child. Katie had to admit that he had loved her deeply during her childhood, and had shown that love in a thousand ways.

"But why did he stay away if he loved me?" she whispered into the empty, dark room. "Why didn't he write, or phone, or—" So many unanswered questions. Was he happy, did he regret leaving her mother...and her, had his new life really been what he wanted? Katie had kept the lid on all those questions and feelings for so long that it was like an opened Pandora's box now. So many things she wanted—no, needed—to know and make right somehow. A resolution was slowly forming in her mind, and when the phone began to ring again she had the crazy notion that it was him, that after all these years her father was calling her.

But it was not her father, it was Will. "Katie?" he said anxiously when she answered. "I've been worried about you."

"You have?" Katie was so glad to hear his voice she kept smiling foolishly into the receiver.

"Yes, I called earlier."

"I tried to catch it, but the phone stopped just as I was unlocking the door."

"You were out with Justin tonight, weren't you?"

"Yes, I was," she said softly.

He waited a moment, then asked, "Are you all right? Did you get things straightened out with him?"

Katie closed her eyes; she thought she could hear the sound of apprehension in his voice. "I told Justin I couldn't marry him, and that I was sorry for playing games all this time."

"Oh, Katie, I'm the one who's sorry. I was pretty rough on you. My own feelings got in the way, honey. It occurred to me after you left the other night that you would never have done any of that deliberately, that the girl I—the girl you are was only doing the best she could. Please forgive me."

Katie gave a shaky laugh. Those same words seemed to be in the air around her tonight. "Will, I ought to thank you instead. There are so many things I see more clearly now. I've been thinking about Eddie—"

"That's another reason I called. We aren't having school on Monday."

"Oh." The word came out tremulously at the thought of what that meant. "Eddie's funeral?"

"Yes. Would you like to go with me? It might be easier than going alone, if we sort of face it together, don't you think?"

"Yes, I do."

There was a long pause, then Will said, "Katie, I've missed you this week."

She tried to sound light, but failed. "I was at the school every day, or didn't you notice?"

"I noticed. But you've been troubled, and I thought I had the right to be righteously angry. By the way, God has reminded me I don't! And I want to see you. Is tomorrow too soon?"

Her heart gave a glad leap at the eagerness in his voice, at the thought of seeing him, but she said slowly, "Will, there's something I have to do, something I can't put off any longer."

"What is it?"

Although the idea had just presented itself a few moments before he called, Katie was convinced of its rightness. "I'm going to visit my father, to make things right between us. It has to be done before I can be free..." She trailed off, not wanting to say, *"Before I can be free to love you."*

"That's a long drive for you to make alone. Or is Sharon going with you?"

"I only just now made up my mind to go," Katie said, laughing a little, "so I haven't even told her."

"Then let me go with you."

Katie felt a lump forming in her throat. "Are you sure you want to? I don't have any idea what I'll be getting into. He might not even want to see me. I haven't called him yet." She sobered; that wouldn't be easy to face.

"I'm going if you are. What time do you want me to pick you up?"

"Is six-thirty too early?"

"I'll be there." There was a pause, then he said, "Are

you going to tell your mother you're going?"

Katie was taken aback. She hadn't thought how her decision might affect Marge. "No, I don't think so, at least not until I see how it turns out."

"That's probably best. Are you going to be all right now? Is Sharon there?"

"No, she's not."

"I hate to think of your being alone. If you want me to come over, I will."

Katie did, very much, but she made herself say, "No, it's late, and we should both get some sleep if we're going to make that long drive tomorrow. I'm sure Sharon will be home soon. But, I can't tell you how much I appreciate your calling and caring."

"I do care, very much, Katie. And I—"

Another awkward silence, and Katie heard herself ask softly, "What were you going to say, Will?"

"I'll tell you later." His voice was gruff as he added, "We'll have plenty of time to talk."

"Yes. Good night, Will."

"Good night, honey."

Katie replaced the receiver gently, thinking how different it seemed when they said good night, not goodbye...wishing he was here beside her. She closed her eyes and knew that he would hold her and kiss her, and she wanted that very much. But she also realized that she must finish the process of understanding and forgiveness that had begun the other night, or she would not be free of all the invisible but powerful things that kept her from being the woman Will deserved.

"Soon," she whispered to the empty room, "soon I'll be free."

As she packed her bag she kept imagining scenes, trying to think of every possible reaction her father could have to seeing her after all this time. Suddenly it occurred to her that she had forgotten to call him, and she went to the phone almost in a daze and dialed information.

"Directory assistance for what city?" came the casual, bored voice.

"Pine Creek, Oregon, or maybe Halfway," said Katie. Squashing a bubble of panic, she repeated the number, then wrote it down. She stared at what she had written a long time before she pushed the buttons with a shaking finger, then waited, not sure she wanted him to answer.

"Hello?"

His voice was the same, and the sound of it made Katie's stomach feel weak. "Hello, Dad, this is Katie—"

"Katie! Where are you?"

She took another deep breath and said, "Oh, I'm still here at school. The perennial student, that's me." She paused, then said, "I want to come and see you."

"You want to come here? When?"

"Tomorrow, if that's all right."

Did he pause, or was it only her imagination, before he said, "Of course it is. Are you coming alone? It's a long drive."

"No, a friend is coming with me." They talked awkwardly for a few moments longer, but when she hung up Katie couldn't remember anything except that she'd asked for directions to his place. And she couldn't remember if he had said I'll be looking for you, or—*we'll* be looking for you. She shrugged and went to finish packing, knowing it would be all right whatever happened and that God would honor her desire to make amends even if she didn't know exactly how—or even if her father would be willing.

Chapter Twelve

By the time they reached Mitchell, Will was almost overwhelmed. "Why didn't someone tell me that Oregon was so...so—"

"Varied?" supplied Katie with a proud little smirk.

"That's a good word, but I think I'd use a stronger one. I had no idea."

They had driven from the fertile, gently rolling farm country of the Willamette Valley over the Cascades—whose Mt. Hood, a peak of over twelve thousand feet, was snow-covered year round—to the high desert country around Bend and Prineville. Will breathed deeply of the sharp, clean, juniper-scented air and reverently pronounced it not unlike his home in Santa Fe.

As they left Mitchell, where they bought juice to accompany the picnic lunch Will had packed as a surprise, Will said, "And you never told me there were so many mountains." He was cautiously navigating the rather narrow two-lane road, which was hemmed in on either side by sharply rising, beautifully colored rock formations.

"Aren't there mountains in New Mexico?"

"There sure are," he answered fervently. "When I was a kid we used to backpack into the Pecos Wilderness." He drove with a casual ease Katie envied. His hands never seemed to clench the wheel, and even the mountain roads, narrow and winding as they were, didn't faze him.

Katie supposed a combination of many things had made him the man he was, and she wondered how he could be such a fascinating blend of focused energy and relaxed, laid-back ease. "I've never been backpacking. Do you think I'd like it?"

"Of course. There's absolutely nothing like being so far from civilization that all you can hear are birds and the wind." He sighed a little, obviously caught up in memories of a special trip. His next words bore that out. "I remember once our family went for a whole week—miraculously everybody managed to get the time off—and spent five days just below Truchas Peak."

Surprised, Katie said, "Your mother, too? My mom is the neatest lady I know, but I can't imagine her without all her special stuff to cook with, and she says nothing could make her give up her own bed."

"I'll bet I could change her mind with a fir-bough bed under the stars," he said with a grin. "My mom especially likes to go, probably because her father worked for the Forest Service all his life and loved the outdoors, too." He carefully edged around a particularly sharp curve. "Did you ever read *The Virginian*?"

"No, I don't think I ever have," said Katie. "Why?"

"Mom read it as a girl, and fell in love with that Virginia gentleman forever."

"So your mother is a romantic," mused Katie.

"She certainly is. Now, my dad is a conservative, conventional man from the word go. Can you imagine his reaction when he asked his demure, petite bride-to-be what she thought of going to one of the better resorts in Arizona for their honeymoon, and she told him she'd rather backpack into the wilderness?"

"You're kidding!" Katie laughed, delighted. "She must be quite a lady." Curiously, even a little shyly, she asked, "Did they go to the resort, or—"

"The wilderness. Mom may be only five-feet-two,

but she usually gets what she wants."

"And did your dad like his unconventional honeymoon?" Somehow the talk of honeymoons with Will made Katie vaguely restless, but very pleasantly so.

"He's still talking about it, thirty-five years later," said Will wryly. "I read *The Virginian* myself, and saw why Mom was so taken with it."

"Why?"

"I'll lend you my copy, so you can see for yourself. Besides being as handsome as they come that Virginia gentleman-turned-cowboy had a definite idea about how he wanted to spend his honeymoon."

"In the mountains?" Katie asked softly.

"Right. There's a scene near the end of the book where you realize how much thought and care he put into sharing his favorite place with his bride that got to me every time I read it. I used to think that's what I'd like, to be alone with the woman I love in the 'haunting sweetness'—as the Virginian called it—of God's high country." He stopped, not because he was embarrassed, but as though he might be uncertain how she had taken his words.

Katie drew a deep breath. She certainly wasn't going to tell Will what she was thinking—or *feeling*. Instead she said, all too aware that Will would know she was changing the subject deliberately, "I can't help but wonder what we'll find when we get to Pine Creek."

He knew all right, but he said, "Want to talk about it? You've been avoiding it ever since we left, but I have a hunch it's been preying on your mind."

Katie admitted uncomfortably to herself that what had been on her mind a few moments before had absolutely nothing to do with her father. "I guess I'm beginning to wonder if it's the right thing to do after all. Maybe I acted hastily."

"How could it be wrong?" He glanced over at her, his eyes taking in her carefully chosen outfit: a creamy cardigan tied loosely around her shoulders, the pale yellow oxford shirt and beige corduroy slacks, that soft halo of hair. "You look especially pretty today, and your dad is going to be proud of the beautiful woman you've grown into."

Though Katie wanted to savor the fact that Will had called her pretty and beautiful in the same sentence, disquiet about her father crowded out any pleasure she felt. "I guess that's part of the problem. It just occurred to me that we're both different people now. I'm not the same any more than he will be," she said, not even trying to hide the anxiety in her voice.

"Hey, hon, you're forgetting that even if he'd never left, even if he'd been around for the past ten years, you both would have changed. People do."

"I know. But if you're there day in and day out, it's not such a shock. And I don't even know if—"

When she didn't continue Will reached over and took one clenched hand in his own. "What were you going to say?"

She didn't answer for a long while. She just stared out the window at the vivid rock formations, the merry river that was running alongside them now. "That's the John Day River. It goes all the way north to the Columbia. You know, until this moment I had forgotten that today is Sunday, Will. Maybe we should go back and find the church in Mitchell. I'm sure there must be one, as small as it is."

"It'll be all right not to go this one time, Katie. I think God will understand. Now come on, out with what's really on your mind."

With a rueful grin she gave up. "The Barbie doll. I never even thought about meeting *her* face to face when I talked to Dad."

"I take it your dad did marry her?"

"Would you believe I don't know? As strange as it seems, when I tell you Mom never talked about him after he left, I mean just that, not one word. And the other night when I was so confused about Justin, and

...you, she opened up some, but not—"

"Not ten years' worth, right?"

"Right. And I was mostly thinking about my own feelings, not Dad's."

"That's as normal as breathing, Katie," said Will easily.

"I suppose so, but it's also pretty selfish. Oh, Will, you've taught me so much. As painful as it was to break things off, I might have strung poor Justin along indefinitely, if it weren't for you."

With a wry grimace Will murmured, "I'm not sure he feels like thanking me. As for teaching you a lot, it's God dealing with you, Katie, not me. He may choose to use me, or your mom, even your dad, maybe, but He's the one who does the teaching."

Katie could watch him as he was speaking because his eyes were on the road. She noticed how strong and capable his hands were on the wheel and remembered how gentle they could be when he held or worked with the babies at school—the way they had felt when he'd caressed her that night on the beach, and in the park. Yes, regardless of how he put it, Will Adams was the teacher.

"Will, I've got a lot of catching up to do, a lot to learn. And something tells me today is going to be one giant step for Kathleen Holland. You'll...help me if it gets sticky, won't you? I'm feeling more afraid the closer we get."

His eyes crinkled with the smile that made her throat tight. "Count on it, honey."

She nodded. "I'm so grateful you called last night. I needed someone badly."

"You were on my mind so strongly I had to call," he said.

"I'm glad," she said softly, "that I was on your mind."

"You are quite a lot." He cleared his throat and said more matter-of-factly, "I'm sort of working on a theory about that."

"What kind of theory?"

"Oh, the idea that if we're open to God's leadership and His promptings, we can make a real difference in other people's lives. Haven't you ever gotten someone on your mind—their name or their face, something—and it just kept coming back?"

"Yes, I have," she said slowly, "but I never thought of it in connection with God."

"It takes on a whole new aspect when you do."

"So you feel that He spoke to you about me last night, and you called because God impressed upon you that I had a need." She frowned slightly, concentrating on the implications of the situation.

"Didn't you?" he asked quietly.

Katie thought of how lonely she'd felt. "Oh, I certainly did."

"And wouldn't you have been a lot more anxious, and afraid of coming alone today?"

"That's putting it mildly. Will, I feel as though I'm on…" She trailed off, then continued resolutely, not caring how it sounded, "on the threshold of an adventure. And not just about my father and setting things straight with him—it's more than that. It's my life as a Christian." There was wonder in her voice as she added, "Why, I'm only a baby!"

"I know the feeling," said Will fervently. "It's not easy, Katie, but it's the most exciting journey we can take."

"A journey," she breathed. Then she gave herself to the silence between them, knowing that his thoughts were like her own. She felt again the stirrings of the most exciting sense of freedom, and it was like a fresh ocean breeze that blew away the fear and anxiety of the unknown day before her.

Pine Creek wasn't really hard to find—at least not after they got on the right road. But until they did, Katie teased Will unmercifully about losing the way twice. She even accused him of doing it on purpose so he could see more of the wonderful, wild country. The second wrong turn led them down a rocky road to such a beautiful spot that they just parked the truck and wandered along the side of a creek. It was still a little too cold from snow run-off for wading, but Katie tried until she was practically blue-footed.

She sat on a flat rock, insisting that it wouldn't take long for her bare feet to dry in the sun. Cottonwood trees lined both sides of the creek bank, their wispy greenery floating in the mild breeze. She could smell summer coming, and some kind of honey-sweet flower was bountifully perfuming the air, probably inciting the bees to riot.

Will, lying beside her with his long legs stretched out, his arms beneath his head, said, "You're putting it off again."

"Me? You're the one who got us lost!" She reached out and tousled his hair, and he caught her hand. When she laughed and tried to pull away she lost her balance and fell against him. The lean hardness of his body was something her own body remembered. And she remembered the fragrant, sun-warmed smell of his freshly laundered cotton shirt, the clean smell of his skin. No aftershave, just...clean man. It made Katie deliciously giddy, and she felt as though she couldn't get close enough to him...and she wanted badly to get closer.

"Katie," he murmured as his arms came slowly, almost hesitantly around her, pulling her to him.

The rushing sound of the little creek was in her ears, but had there been no water nearby she thought perhaps she still would have heard that roaring as his hands moved slowly from her shoulders to her waist and drew her even nearer. Hardly realizing what she was doing, Katie left tiny, butterfly light kisses on his neck, his jaw, the side of his mouth, until her lips touched his, then touch was no longer enough. She felt as though she was drowning. She wanted to drown in the whirlpool of his kiss.

Suddenly, almost roughly, he pushed her away, holding her at arm's length. "Don't, Katie."

She stared down at him. "What...what do you mean?"

Will sat up, and moved a bit away from her. "It's not right, not now."

"Not right?" Katie's voice was cold and small. She'd never allowed herself to be as free and open, to show affection to anyone as she just had. To have him reject it was very painful. She stood up, dusted her slacks off, straightened her hair.

Slowly he rose and looked steadily down at her, his eyes troubled. "I've hurt you. I'm sorry—"

"No need to be sorry, you didn't do anything." As she walked away from him she thought, *No, you didn't, and that's what hurts!* If she hadn't been so mortified she'd have thought the whole thing was funny...the poor big man having to fight off the too-eager woman.

When he reached the truck she was sitting stiffly on her side, looking out the window as though there were a parade going by, instead of a blank canyon wall. "Katie, let me explain," he began, but she cut him off.

"Will, I'd rather you didn't. We'd better get going. It's been a long day already, and as you pointed out I still have to face my father, and who knows what else." She met his eyes now, gave him a cool smile, then turned away and missed the look of troubled uncertainty on his face.

She didn't speak again until they had gotten back on the right road and were approaching the weathered sign proclaiming Pine Creek, Pop. 79. To the left was a large wooden building that seemed to house a garage, a service station, the post office and a general store, as well as a bar.

Still feeling as though her face was made of cardboard, Katie said, "Dad's place is down by the creek, in that mobile home park across the highway. It's the one at the very end." She remembered with a jolt of sadness that the House at the beach was at the end of the road, too. But more than a whole state separated them. She was wishing that she'd never started this day, and she knew if she had come alone she would turn around right now and head for home.

But one look at Will's square, firm jaw made her certain that even if she insisted he would not leave. He would see that she went through with it. Far from feeling admiration for him, she felt only a slow, burning resentment which stemmed from the painful scene by the creek a while ago. Suddenly she knew she wasn't ready to face her father.

"Will, wait! please stop—"

He glanced at her sharply. "What?"

"I said please stop the car!"

"But, why?"

"I need..." Her words ended in a ragged sob, and she looked pleadingly at him through tears.

He pulled the truck over to the side of the road and cut the engine. "What do you need, honey?" The sharpness was gone now.

"I thought I was fine, but I'm not."

He nodded slowly, and put his hands out. She put her own into them, and immediately she felt his warm strength, saw the compassion in his eyes. Softly he said, "I could do it for you, but it would be best if we both prayed, together."

She nodded, then bowed her head. For a long moment she just breathed very deeply, not thinking at all, feeling that silent warm strength flowing into her from Will's hands. And the prayer was not uttered aloud, it went from her heart. *"Oh, Lord, I believe that what I've set out to do is right. Give me courage instead of this awful fear, and settle my spirit so I can face Dad with calmness and he can...see You instead of just me."*

This last thought was a new one for Katie, and through it God prepared her for the time that followed. She could forget herself and concentrate on her father and on her reason for coming—to make things right again. Katie raised her head to find herself looking directly into Will's blue eyes. She smiled. "I'm ready now."

His own smile was warm. "I do believe you are." As he started the engine and eased around the last curve in the road he said casually, "That must be him waiting for you."

Surprised at the eagerness she suddenly felt, Katie leaned forward. Yes, it was him. Her throat felt tight as she saw that he was much thinner than she remembered, and she'd certainly never seen him dressed as he was now. From this distance he seemed to be ten years younger, not older. She remembered what he'd said about not getting old.

He wore a battered Greek fisherman's hat at a rakish angle, his white shirt was open deep at the throat, and the faded Levi's were as snug as a teenager's. But as she stepped from the truck and walked slowly toward him, Katie could see the permanent deep dent between his brows and the sun-wrinkles at the corners of his eyes. Not so young after all. The years were there, and a certain sadness even when he smiled.

"Katie."

She faltered at the sound of her name. Was it her imagination? Was it only because she wanted so badly for him to be glad to see her, or was he just trying to make the best of a difficult situation? But then he held out his arms and she went straight into them.

He held her tight for a long moment, then laughed shakily. "I wasn't sure why you were coming. Oh, I thought a lot of things. Didn't sleep much after you called last night, trying to figure out why you decided to come now." He smiled down at her, still holding her to his side with one arm as he extended his hand to

Will, standing quietly nearby. "Kenneth Holland, and you're—"

"Will Adams." His eyes took Katie's father's measure as surely as his own was being taken.

With his free hand Kenneth made a sweeping gesture. "Well, Katie, this is it, what the last ten years of my life have been poured into." Too late he stopped, realizing that at least part of those ten years should have been given to his only child. But he went on pointing things out, and Will and Katie followed.

He showed them the building that housed equipment for his tourist guide service, explaining with disappointment keen in his voice that the man from whom he'd bought the business had assured him he'd be able to continue running the river. But the man had neglected to inform him that the Forest Service would probably file an injunction to keep him off the river indefinitely. There was a lot of legal mumbo jumbo, but in the meantime he wasn't allowed to act as a guide on the increasingly popular raft trips down the Snake River.

He shrugged. "I pick up a bit here and there running a shuttle service for the other guides, and I've been selling a few articles to sports magazines and some of those new back-to-nature things."

"You're a writer?" Will asked. "Katie never mentioned that."

They were standing in front of a thriving garden. Kenneth gave that slow smile. "I'm surprised she told you about me at all." Then he said, "I used to do some technical writing when I was working for…before I came here. But my life consists of hunting and fishing, and acting as guide for people who pay, very well, I might add, for a knucklehead like me to kowtow to them, and then I write about the mighty hunter's experiences. And I garden."

He knelt in the sandy loam and plucked one lonesome weed. "It's not a gentleman's hobby. I wouldn't eat very well if it wasn't for my cabbage patch," he added honestly. He stood up then and put his hands on his hips. "But I've a notion you didn't come clear across the state to hear me spout off about my cabbages."

Katie had been watching him closely, never taking her eyes off him, wondering at the lack of bitterness in her. It had been a part of her so long she felt almost naked without it—naked, or perhaps just open and vulnerable. He was not the same man she remembered at all. The man she'd hated for the past ten years had been a prosperous, dissatisfied, selfish man who thought only of himself, who wanted freedom from his wife and his child at any price. This man had paid the price all right, perhaps even more than he owed.

She was surprised that all she felt for him was a gentle sort of curiosity, a need to know him as he was now. Quietly she said, "No, Dad, you're wrong. That's just why we did come—to see how you are, what you're doing."

The look in Kenneth Holland's eyes was one of such stunned, humble gratitude that Will turned away from it, obviously feeling he was intruding. "I need to stretch my legs. Think I'll take a walk." He squeezed Katie's shoulder briefly. "Be back in a bit, honey," he said, then strolled down to the nearby creek which was boisterously, joyously making its way around the bend where Kenneth's small mobile home sat.

For a few minutes neither Katie nor her father spoke. Finally he said, "He seems to be a fine young man."

"He is," she agreed softly.

"I've missed so much." The regret was there—he didn't try to hide it—regret that he had missed her growing up, missed seeing her become a young woman.

"Dad, there's something I have to ask you."

A quick look of consternation flashed on his lean, sun-bronzed face, but he met her eyes without flinching. "Anything, Katie, anything."

"I want...I *need* your forgiveness."

He frowned. "What could there possibly be for me to forgive you for? You certainly didn't do anything wrong. It was me—I'm the one who left and who hurt you so terribly."

For a moment Katie forgot everything but those first lonely years before she'd built the barriers. Before she could stop them the words tumbled out. "Why didn't you ever come back to see me, or write, or *anything*?"

He sighed, not looking at her, his eyes following Will's meandering progress along the creek. "I told myself it would be less complicated—that you would be less confused about things if I just stayed away. But I guess it's closer to the truth to say I was afraid to face you. And the longer I stayed away the easier it seemed." He rubbed his temple slowly as though his head ached. "After what I did to your mother I knew she didn't want to see me again. I don't blame her."

"For a long time I thought you were cruel and unbelievably selfish," Katie said gently, "and that's why I want your forgiveness—because I hated you so much."

"You had every right to hate me." His voice was heavy and low.

She caught his arm. "No, Dad, don't you see, I don't have the right to hate you. No matter what you did, I need to forgive you. And I have now, and you have to say you forgive me, so…so we can eat supper because I'm about to starve to death!" She laughed breathlessly.

Startled, he looked at her closely and began to laugh too. "Of course I do, if that's what you want!" He hugged her as she turned to him. It wasn't exactly clear whether they were laughing or crying. Will must have heard them for he came back, a wary look on his face until he saw the tension seemed to have gone away completely.

"Come inside, Will, before Katie wastes away from hunger!" He held her at arm's length. "She looks as though she has a way to go, but we'd better feed her just in case." He put his arm around her shoulders as they walked toward the mobile home, which was surrounded by a spectacular assortment of spring flowers.

Fleetingly Katie remembered her fears about the Barbie doll when she saw the flowers, as well as when they entered the tidy, compact livingroom and were assailed by the spicy aroma of something Italian simmering in the kitchen.

Kenneth must have seen her anxiety as she glanced around. He said quietly, "You can relax, Katie. Barbara left before the first year was up, and there hasn't been anyone else. If you're wondering why everything is so neat, well—after a while of living in a pigsty a man just gets the idea it's better to keep things in their place. I've even learned to cook, but I'll certainly never match your mother."

She knew from his smile that immense relief must have shown on her face. "I'd be lying if I said I was sorry she's gone, Dad."

"So don't, I'm not. It was a mistake—a bad one in a lot of ways." He motioned for Will to sit down at the kitchen table, set for three. "Remember that, Will, when you get forty and foolish."

Will, who'd been almost shyly staying in the background, nodded thoughtfully. "Mid-life crisis. Isn't it supposed to come from getting to the place in life where you look back and things haven't gone like you'd planned, or hoped—"

"And you look forward and can't see it getting any better," finished Kenneth. He was peering into the oven at the bubbling casserole. "Lasagna. Is that okay with everyone?" Will and Katie both agreed enthusiastically, and after Kenneth told her to take the salad from the refrigerator he asked, "What do you do, Will? Something that will keep you challenged past those fitful forties, I hope?"

Will's quiet shyness disappeared as, over a simple but very tasty dinner he enthused about his kids, making it plain that he felt Katie was a natural with them as well.

Later when they were sitting outside in the soft twilight by the creek, Kenneth said to Katie, "So you plan to make a career of teaching children who are—what was the term Will used?"

"Developmentally disabled." Katie listened contentedly to the creek's conversation—it was almost as though it were a fourth person among them. "Yes, I believe it's what I've been looking for. Don't you remember how I used to moan about not ever being good at anything?"

Kenneth chuckled. "I remember. And this you're good at, working with these kids?"

"She's very good," said Will. "And believe me, not everyone can do it. It takes a very special kind of person."

His voice, saying those words that meant so much to Katie, made her shiver. "I'll have to go to school more. I've wasted so much time and Mom's money, too. She kept telling me that she wanted me to go to college because she hadn't."

Kenneth waited a bit before he asked, "Has your mother remarried, Katie?"

She couldn't see his face, but she read the wistfulness in his tone. "No, Dad. She doesn't even date, never has."

"I hurt her too deeply for her to trust anyone again, I'm afraid." It wasn't wistfulness in his voice now—it was contrite, painful remorse.

Not able to deny it, Katie said, "She has a nice little catering business, and when she feels like it there are always lucky people who'll pay the going rate for bed and breakfast. Holland House and Mom's soup are always in demand."

Her father said hesitantly, "Does she know you came here?"

"No, I didn't tell her. I...wasn't sure what we'd find."

In the poignant silence that followed, the rushing,

merry creek spoke its mind. The spring run-off had swelled it to a chorus.

After a while Kenneth said, "You know, sometimes I sort of close one ear and pretend the sound I hear is the ocean, but not often." Again, sadness was faintly audible in his tone. "You'll stay the night, of course. I have an extra room, the bed's all made—" He stopped, then doggedly went on. "Look, I know things are different these days. If you two have been…if you're—"

"No, sir, we're not," interrupted Will firmly. "If you have an extra sleeping bag, I'd really enjoy sleeping out here. You're right about one thing, that creek sounds marvelous."

Katie listened to Will's definite, *this is the way it is, sir, there's nothing between me and your daughter* attitude, and after what had happened that afternoon she wondered what, if anything at all, was between her and Will. She wanted to go to him and say, *"Let's talk. Let's go for a walk along this beautiful creek and pretend it's the ocean, like Dad does, and let it help straighten things out."*

But she didn't, and not long after she was fighting sleep, trying to mull over the eventful day. With an aching longing she thought of the moments in Will's arms this afternoon. What had she wanted him to do, anyway? She told herself he'd acted in an honorable way, that there was no other way he could have acted. But she also wondered if the reason he'd drawn away from her was honor, or if he simply did not feel as intensely about her as she did about him. Katie made herself face that possibility, as little as she wanted to.

The sleepless night before, the long, anxious day, and the strange sensation of being under her father's roof—even if it was a tiny trailer and she could see a water stain in the shape of a beagle's head in one corner of the room—took its toll. The last thing she remembered was a prayer of thankfulness—for what she trusted God to see in her heart, and for His will to be done in her life.

Chapter Thirteen

Katie had known, even before she heard Will tell her father the evening they all sat beside Pine Creek, that she had finally found the special niche where she fit. It was with her kids. As the term drew to a close she worked harder at her other classes, knowing that in time she would be grateful for a degree. She was more certain than ever that, hard work or not, it really was the best thing for her life at this particular moment.

A week after she and Will returned from Pine Creek she received a letter from her father, thanking her for caring enough to come and saying somewhat vaguely that he'd been doing a lot of thinking since they left. About what, he didn't say. Katie mulled it over and came to several possible conclusions—that he was tired of being alone and wanted to reconcile with her mother being the most fanciful. Sternly she told herself there was nothing whatever in his letter, no matter how many times she reread it, that even remotely hinted at such a conclusion, and still she hoped.

The month of May was almost gone, and the term would be over in two days. She had, she thought smugly, done fairly well on all her exams. It was even a bit easier now. She still was no more of a student than ever, but when she felt as though she would rather leap a tall building at a single bound than write another term paper, she'd whisper, "It's for the kids, Katie." For Katie's Kids. That's what everyone who knew her called them now, because she talked of little else.

Today was the last session at the preschool, and all the parents were coming at noon for a potluck meal. Everything was really going well for Katie—except for Will's quiet, distant attitude. Katie kept telling herself she was much too proud to approach him first. She even believed it most of the time and acted accordingly. But she couldn't keep from indulging Sharon in her urge to speculate.

The two of them were on Katie's bed, a bag of Oreos—her breakfast—in Sharon's lap. Sharon was saying, "Maybe he's the kind of guy who likes to make all the moves, and you stepped over the line."

"Oh, Sharon, do you really think a man like Will would be that—" She stopped, trying to marshal her thoughts, then sighed. "It's hard living in a transition time."

"What do you mean, transition?" Sharon took another Oreo, carefully pulled it apart and ate all the frosting before she started on the cookie. It was her ritual, and it never varied.

The look in Katie's eyes was pensive. "Oh, just that for a long time women have had to wait for a man to declare his feelings first, never mind what *she* feels."

"Safer that way," mumbled Sharon around a cookie.

"Yes, that's true. It's also true that a lot of women are beginning to think that maybe we should take some of the initiative in our relationships, some of the risks."

"Do *you* believe that?" Sharon asked, eyes narrowed shrewdly.

"I'm not sure what I believe. But when you think of how men are on the line all the time, it doesn't seem right. Maybe we've been too safe."

"Exactly what are you leading up to?" She shook her shaggy, freshly sheared hair—she'd gotten Katie up early yesterday morning to pass judgment on it—and said, "No, let me guess. You've decided Will Adams may never ah, how did you put it, declare himself, so you're trying to persuade yourself it's okay for you to do it instead. Am I right?"

"Pretty much," admitted Katie sheepishly.

"Well, what's the problem? Or aren't you sure how you feel about him after all?"

Katie got such a woebegone look on her face that Sharon clucked with sympathy now. "I'm sure about me, but not him, Sharon. It's been three weeks since we visited with my dad, and Will treats me the way he did the first three weeks we met, when he thought I was a nitwit."

Impishly Sharon said, "Could be he knows you're one now!"

For an answer Katie threw a pillow at her. "Be serious! It hurts working with him every day, being polite and helpful, acting as though I'm just another volunteer."

"Oh, I've got the feeling he thinks of you as more than just a volunteer." She ate one last cookie and rolled the bag shut. "A *lot* more than just a volunteer."

Katie rose, strode to her closet, and stood glaring moodily at her clothes. "I'm not so sure any more, from the way he's acting. And I always thought it was my job as a woman to make him wonder. Will doesn't play by the same rules that—" She stopped, too late.

"That Justin did?" said Sharon slyly.

Katie scowled at being caught, and yanked out a pale yellow blouse with a dainty embroidered handkerchief set diagonally into the front of it.

"Pretty," said Sharon, all demure sweetness now.

"Yes, but will it do any good? He probably won't even notice what I'm wearing."

"Katie..." Sharon began, then trailed off.

"What?" Her voice was muffled as she pulled the blouse on over her head.

"This isn't easy to say, but I'm your friend, right?"

"Go ahead," said Katie, seeing that Sharon's mood had changed completely.

"You have to believe that even if Will never 'declares himself', you can make it fine."

"Can I?" Katie whispered.

"Yes. Justin really loved you and he's going to be fine. Didn't you tell me you heard that he got his promotion and is dating a woman in his office?" Katie nodded wordlessly. "And you'll have your kids, regardless of what happens."

Katie stood still for a long moment then said slowly, "Yes, I'll have my kids. You're right, of course. Thank you, roomie." She went over to Sharon, who allowed a brief hug before she wriggled away.

"Good grief," she said in embarrassment. "Get ready, or you're going to be late."

Katie took her advice and went to school with a lighter step than she had for days. She still caught herself looking for Eddie, and knew it would be a long time before the ache eased when she thought of him. She faced the fact that each one of the children would have a very special place in her heart forever, no matter how long she was actually able to be with them.

Robby had finally begun to speak. He tried so hard. Some sounds still evaded him, for instance, he could say m's and n's but l's and y's seemed impossible. It made her proud, happy, and wrenched her heart all at the same time to watch him struggle and fail as often as he succeeded. But Robby wasn't the only one with tenacity. She came to the conclusion that the courage these children inevitably showed could make a difference in her own attitude. She came to another rather humbling conclusion—a teacher always learns more than she teaches.

All of the children felt the excitement of closing day, and parents started arriving early with covered dishes and gelatin salads and desserts for the potluck to be held afterward. It was Katie's and Ellen's job to help set up the tables outside and as they directed the mothers, a few fathers, brothers and sisters, Ellen said, "You know, Katie, a lot of our kids have one advantage that normal children don't always have."

A little startled, Katie looked up from the stack of flimsy plastic flatware she was trying, without much success, to arrange. "What on earth would that be?"

"Oh, the fact that most of the parents have this fierce attitude that says, 'No matter how awful or hard the handicap, these are our children and we'll do whatever is necessary to see that they become all they can be.' "

"That's true, isn't it," Katie said thoughtfully, raising her face to the welcome warmth of the sun for a moment. "I suppose a lot of times parents of normal kids don't even begin to tap their enormous potential because—"

"Because they're normal, and they don't bother," finished Ellen.

Katie watched Ellen for a moment, then said something that had come to her mind more than once during the term. "Ellen, have you ever thought of becoming a teacher?"

Ellen laughed. "Me? I'd never make it through college!"

"Listen, if *I* can—and I'm going to—anybody can!" She laughed too, then said seriously, "You'd make a fine teacher."

"Do you really think so?" There was a note of yearning in her voice.

"There's no doubt in my mind. I think you should talk to Will about it, and Dr. Johnson, and—"

Ellen held up her hands. "Wait a minute, one step at a time! First I have to talk to my husband—"

Before she could finish they were interrupted, and it was time for lunch. But Katie felt a glow of satisfaction at having had a part, however small, in Ellen's becoming aware of her potential.

The weather was perfect, sunny and clear. With Stacy

in her arms, Katie watched Will circulate among the parents. Although she couldn't hear what he was saying, she knew he had encouraging, optimistic words for each, especially those whose children would be going on to public schools next year.

As she took the opportunity to gaze at him, the thought uppermost in her mind was not about the children at all, but whether or not she had the courage to invite him to the beach for the weekend. She kept thinking about it throughout the meal and the goodbyes, and the inevitable cleanup. Finally it was done and as it had happened so often in the past few months, she was the only one left besides Will.

He was standing at the window when she came in with the last chairs that had been taken outside. His hands were tucked into the back pockets of his jeans—new in honor of the potluck, maybe—a melancholy look on his lean face.

"You'll miss the ones who're not coming back next year, won't you?" she asked softly.

He nodded, allowing himself one huge sigh before he turned and started sorting the papers and folders on his desk. "I can't help but worry when I know all the pitfalls waiting for them out there."

She smiled. "If you worry this much about the kids here, think how you'll be when you have children of your own—" She stopped, suddenly acutely aware of how different she felt saying those words than when she'd said something similar to Justin. Then it had been simply Justin's children; now she realized she wanted very much for Will's children to be hers, too.

"You're right," he agreed wryly. "I'll probably be the kind of father teachers hate, always fretting and stewing over his kids."

"Oh, maybe not." With the definite feeling of walking on uncharted waters, she said as casually as she could, "Are you going to be busy this weekend?"

He looked up at her, his face thoughtful, serious. "Yes, I have plans."

Katie's heart plummeted, but she said with a very bright smile, "Oh, you do, that's good." *Stupid thing to say, Katie, really stupid.* Her inner self replied, *"Well, what do you want me to say?"*

Will was watching her now, the hint of a smile on his face. "I hope it's good. What I had in mind was calling up a friend of mine, yours, too, as a matter of fact, and asking her if she has anyone coming for bed and breakfast this weekend. If not, I'll make a reservation."

Katie could see the glint in his blue eyes. "Will Adams, you knew all along what I was planning to ask!"

He nodded. "Then why did you wait so long to say anything? Why did you let me make a fool of myself?"

"Is that the way you felt?" he asked curiously.

"Well, yes. Have you got any idea how much nerve it took for me to ask you?"

"You bet I do, honey. Any male over the age of fourteen knows exactly how much nerve it takes."

"That's something else I wanted to talk to you about."

"What," he asked mischievously, "fourteen-year-old boys?"

"No, no, about men and women and roles, and who should do what, and—"

"Whoa! You've just outlined a year or two of discussions." The look in his eyes changed to that intense, serious look that made her feel short of breath. "And there are a couple of things we need to discuss that take priority over the way fourteen-year-old boys feel, anyway."

"Mom is keeping the whole weekend free for us."

"Pretty sure of yourself, aren't you?" He came over to her, not touching her, but close enough to.

"Oh, Will, no. I'm not." She wanted so badly for him to take her in his arms she could almost taste it.

But he didn't. He just smiled and said, "Your car or mine?"

"Mine takes less gas."

"Right. I like a woman who makes things easier for a man."

"I'll remember that."

"Does three o'clock sound good?"

"Fine. I'll pick you up then."

He went back to the job of clearing his desk, and Katie realized he didn't intend to talk any more. She suppressed a sigh and murmured something about seeing him later. When he barely responded she left, thinking Justin might be a better man than she imagined to have been so patient for so long, especially if he'd felt a tenth of the impatience she felt now.

It was only two hours from the time Katie left Will at the school until three, when he said he'd be ready to leave, but she was ready long before then, and prowling around the apartment restlessly.

Sharon, having extracted all the details about the coming weekend that she could pry out of a preoccupied Katie, said confidently, "Stop worrying. It's going to work out, Katie, you'll see."

"Oh, Sharon, I just can't be sure." She stood at the window as she had so often, seeing and not really seeing the rich green of the trees which were fully leafed out now. The lushness of their fulfilled promise gave her an obscure hope. "He had thought of going to Mom's too, but—"

"Roomie, you're the neatest girl I've ever known, and if Will Adams doesn't see it, what do you need with a numb-brain like that?"

Her face was full of affection and Katie had to swallow hard to answer. "I don't know, but I know I need him." This time it was the unaffectionate Sharon who came over and gave Katie a quick, hard hug.

"Now go on." She flashed a gap-toothed grin as Katie left, waving from the door.

The conversation during the drive to Lincoln City was mainly about the children and Will's hopes and fears for those who were going on. When Marge, waiting for them on the porch, asked how things had gone Katie dredged up a quick smile, left Will to answer, and went to unpack.

She was surprised to see her mother at the door of her room a few moments later. "Hi, Mom, where's Will?"

Marge looked around at the familiar chaos that invaded the room every time Katie came home. "I think he's caught your need for a walk on the beach first thing. He's really wound up about school, isn't he?"

"That's putting it mildly. It seems to be all he thinks about." She was sitting in a wicker chaise lounge in front of the low, wide window with its breathtaking, bird's-eye view of the water.

Marge came over and stood at the window, but she turned to look at her daughter rather than the view. "And you have other things on your mind, things you'd like to discuss with him, I can see."

Katie looked a little abashed, but not much. "You're right, Mom. But he's so—"

"One-track?" When Katie nodded woefully she laughed. "A lot of men are like that, Katie. Single-minded. But they get things done."

With her knees drawn up, her chin resting on them, Katie said softly, "You got my letter about Justin?"

"Yes. Was it the right move? Are you sure now that some time has passed?"

"I'm sure. Just as sure as I am that Will is right for me."

"I can live with that," said Marge lightly, "with no problems at all. But I can also see there's something that's not exactly the way it should be. What is it, Katie?" She pulled up the armless rocker that she'd rocked Katie in when she was a baby.

When she spoke again Katie's voice was not much more than a whisper. "There've been a few times that I thought Will felt just the same as I do. But I'm not sure any more. And I can't decide whether or not I should tell him how I feel before he—"

"Before he tells you he loves you?" her mother asked gently.

"Yes."

"Oh, Katie, you've gone past the time when I can give you a pat answer. This is one thing you'll have to decide for yourself."

Katie looked into her mother's calm eyes, and before she could think whether or not it was the right thing to do she said, "Mom, Will and I went to Pine Creek...and saw him."

"Your father," she said, her face showing the surprise Katie heard in her soft tone.

"I...had to. Does that upset you? Oh, I hope not!"

"Why..." She was frowning—not angrily, but still sort of disbelieving. For a moment she stared at Katie, her lower lip caught in her teeth. Then she said, "No, it doesn't upset me. I'm a little surprised, though. How did it go?"

"Pretty well. It was something I had to do, Mom."

"I understand, really I do."

Katie sprang up and hugged her tightly. "He asked about you. And that girl left just months after he...they..."

"It's all right, Katie. I made my own peace with it years ago."

Once again Katie was aware she might be rushing in where angels wouldn't be caught, but she said, her face against her mother's shoulder, "Mom, could you ever...do you think you could ever live with Dad again?"

The reply was so long in coming Katie thought perhaps Marge was angry. She had stiffened and drawn away slightly. "I don't know, Katie. The only way I've been able to survive is to close off that part of myself, not to let myself even—"

"Feel?" Katie asked, twisting around to see into her

face. "Mom, you can't go forever not feeling."

Marge's smile was small and sad. "I might, Katie."

"But if he were to—"

Gently, firmly, Marge interrupted her. "A while ago I said you'd gotten to the place where I had to let you make your own decisions. Don't you think it would be a good idea if you gave me the same privilege?"

Katie sighed. She was right, of course. "Okay, Mom. Do you suppose Will has had enough time to blow all his cobwebs away?"

"Probably. I told him you'd be along shortly."

Katie hugged her again. "We'll be back in time to eat. What's for supper?"

"Minestrone. It's the special at Angelo's this weekend. Just call me Mama Angelo." She touched her daughter's cheek. "You'll be all right, Katie, don't worry. If Will doesn't see what an outstanding partner you'd make, who needs him?"

"That's what Sharon said," Katie replied with a grimace. "Thanks, Mom."

There was a brisk wind blowing from the south, and with it a few clouds that could mean rain, but Katie thought maybe not. She wandered north, not sure which way he might have gone. She was perhaps two miles up the beach before she saw him, walking slowly, coming toward her. With an effort she slowed her own steps. A funny image, probably from some sentimental old movie, imposed itself on her mind: a girl with long, flowing hair and wearing a white dress, running toward a man whose arms were outstretched.

She was still grinning at that thought when he drew close and said, "What in the world are you thinking about?"

"You," she said honestly.

"And thinking about me makes you look like you just heard a good joke?"

"I guess so." He looked so much more relaxed than he had earlier she had trouble keeping herself from reaching up and stroking his cheek. "You look better."

"Amazing what sea air will do. I understand it used to be a cure even doctors prescribed."

"My kind of doctor," said Katie, falling into step as he began walking again. She thought of and discarded several possible ways to say what was on her mind. Finally she caught his arm and stopped. "Will, there's something I have to tell you." He looked at her, and she tried to decide exactly what was in his eyes.

"What is it, Katie?"

With a sense of throwing caution completely to the winds, of burning her bridges behind her, of every such cliche she'd ever heard, she said very, very, softly, "I love you."

Will stared at her for so long, not speaking, that she grew cold and afraid. He must have seen it in her face, for just as she was about to turn and run away he held out his arms and she leaned into his embrace slowly, as though there was a wind at her back, which there was.

He held her tightly, and she felt him kiss her hair once, lightly. Then, his voice low, he said, "Oh, Katie, I love you, too."

"You do?" She pulled away to stare up at him, her eyes wide and glistening. "Then why have you been so far away all this time? Ever since we came back from Pine Creek…" Suddenly she was a little mad. "And by the way, why did you push me away that day? You didn't act as though you loved me then—"

He stopped her words with a tender kiss that soon became a different kind of kiss altogether. Katie gave herself completely to the ecstasy that filled her, that wildfire she'd felt before and was not afraid of now.

When she could speak she breathed, *"Why?"*

"Why did I keep my distance?"

She nodded, thinking how good and fresh he smelled.

"Because I thought you needed time."

"Time for what?"

"To be absolutely certain about Justin, for one thing," he said gravely.

"But I told you—"

"I know what you told me. And it wasn't that I didn't believe you. I just felt you needed to work through it completely. Two years is a long time to be involved with someone." He stroked her cheek, traced her mouth with a gentle finger. "And then there was the business with your father. Whether you knew it or not, all that took a great deal of emotional strength."

"Then you were just thinking of me? Of giving me time?"

Will looked away, then back, meeting her eyes. "Katie, I'd like to be able to say yes to that question. But I can't."

He looked so serious that Katie felt a stab of panic. "Why not, Will? Tell me."

"It might be easier to say if we're walking."

"All right," she said in a frightened little voice.

"Don't sound so—"

"Scared? I can't help it, I am."

"Of what?"

"Of finding out you don't want me the way I want you."

"Oh, Katie, you're wonderful!" He laughed, delighted.

"How wonderful?" she asked, throwing her arms around his neck.

"Wonderful enough that I want to spend the rest of my life loving you," he answered, his words muffled in her hair.

"Do you mean that?" She drew back to look into his eyes.

"Would I lie?"

It was her turn to laugh. "Not with those true-blue eyes! Then what in the world were you talking about?"

"Before I met you, Katie, I had it in my head that marriage might not be for me."

Pertly she said, "Well, if you're planning to spend the rest of your life with me, you'll have to think *that* over."

He grinned. "You're right, and I did. But there's a lot involved, Katie. You've seen how I am with the kids. They take a lot out of me, and I want to give it. I'm afraid I have to give it."

"But isn't there enough love in you for me, too?" she asked softly.

He kissed her forehead and she nestled close again. "Yes, but I didn't know that. I thought it would be unfair to ask a woman to put up with me. I'm a hard man to put up with, honey. I had to be sure you wanted to."

"Oh, I want to." Katie was glad beyond words they were on the beach. The vast sky and endless water seemed to be a reflection of the possibilities of their love. "I can think of only one problem we might have trouble solving," she said, forcing herself to look serious.

"Tell me, I'll solve it. The way I feel right now, nothing seems impossible." He wasn't looking at the sky and water, he was gazing into her eyes.

His lips were leaving a soft, shivering trail from her eyebrow to her ear, but she managed to say, "A classic problem—the seashore or the mountains." The expression on his face was the same as Katie felt—slightly dazed. "Where will we spend our honeymoon? I couldn't get *The Virginian* out of my mind after that tale you told about their honeymoon in God's high country. I always thought I wanted to be here, but—"

"How about both?"

"Could we?" she asked eagerly.

"Katie, we can do anything we want!" He caught her close, so close she was almost satisfied; then he said, his voice slightly different now, "There's one more thing, and this decision will have to be mostly up to you."

"What, Will?" she asked, as sure as he'd been that regardless of what it was, she could do it.

Carefully he said, "I don't want to teach at the college forever."

"That's all right. But what else would you do?"

"Have a school in my—our home," he said, watching her face closely.

"You mean right in the house?"

"Yes, how would you feel about that?"

"Fine. Why not?"

"Because I've got an idea not many women would like that. You amaze me."

"Why on earth would that amaze you? It's a perfectly good idea. We could have a big house, maybe one with a huge daylight basement for the school. And when we have our own kids it would be a good experience for them, you know, learning tolerance and all that. And from what I've read it's good for kids with problems to be around normal kids. And I'd rather be at home instead of having to go out to work." She paused for a breath and added, "But I'll have to finish school for sure now, because it would be so much better if both of us are accredited teachers, don't you think?"

"I think you've probably just done enough talking for both of us for the entire weekend, so now we have to think of something else to do."

She twined her arms around his neck and pulled his head slowly down. "I know just the thing."

Before his lips touched hers he murmured, "Oh, Katie, I love you."

"And I love you, teacher."

Other Thomas Nelson Romances you will enjoy

Shirley Sanders
SONG OF TANNEHILL [No. 6]
Holly Scott sees Luke Westford as an arrogant stranger intruding on her Alabama homeland—until she realizes there's more to him than his job as a Washington official indicates.
ISBN 0-8407-7356-0, **$2.25**

Marylin Young
THE HEART OF THE STORM [No. 5]
Galveston legal secretary Melanie Hart and her employer Bret Stone, the man she loves, fight to save her ancestral home from land developers—and themselves from a deadly hurricane.
ISBN 0-8407-7354-4, **$2.25**

Jane Peart
LOVE TAKES FLIGHT [No. 4]
Trying to deny her love for playboy pilot T. J. Lang, Roblynn Mallory is forced to reevaluate her feelings when he is caught in a dangerous mid-air hijacking.
ISBN 0-8407-7353-6, **$2.25**

Irene Brand
A CHANGE OF HEART [No. 3]
Against her better judgment, teller Ginger Wilson is attracted to bank-owner Darren Banning, but she realizes a future with him is hopeless unless she unlocks the astonishing secret from his past.
ISBN 0-8407-7352-8, **$2.25**

Anna Lloyd Staton
THE CHALLENGED HEART [No. 2]
New York-based editor of a successful magazine, Cassandra Delaney falls for her wealthy boss—until she visits Kentucky horse country and meets a dedicated country doctor who challenges her big-city values.
ISBN 0-8407-7361-7, **$2.25**

Patricia Dunaway
IRISH LACE [No. 1]
When Texas-born Brenna Ryan embarks on a vacation to Ireland, the last thing she expects to do is fall in love with brooding Dr. Michael Larkin and attempt to change his attitude toward women.
ISBN 0-8407-7350-1, **$2.25**

Dear Reader:

I am committed to bringing you the kind of romantic novels you want to read. Please fill out the brief questionnaire below so we will know what you like most in romance.

Mail to: Etta Wilson
Thomas Nelson Publishers
P.O. Box 141000
Nashville, Tenn. 37214

1. Why did you buy this inspirational romance?

   ☐ Author
   ☐ Back cover description
   ☐ Christian story
   ☐ Cover art
   ☐ Recommendation from others
   ☐ Title
   ☐ Other_____

2. What did you like best about this book?

   ☐ Heroine
   ☐ Hero
   ☐ Christian elements
   ☐ Setting
   ☐ Story Line
   ☐ Secondary characters

3. Where did you buy this book?

   ☐ Christian bookstore
   ☐ Supermarket
   ☐ Drugstore
   ☐ General bookstore
   ☐ Book Club
   ☐ Other (specify)_____

4. Are you interested in buying other romances in this series?

   ☐ Very interested ☐ Somewhat interested
   ☐ Not interested

5. Please indicate your age group.
   ☐ Under 18 ☐ 25-34
   ☐ 18-24 ☐ 35-49 ☐ Over 50

6. Comments or suggestions?

7. Would you like to receive a free copy of the our romance newsletter? If so, please fill in your name and address.

Name _____

Address _____

City _____ State _____ Zip _____

7357-9